Penguin Books

Limelight and ⟨

Claire Bloom was born in London. A professional actress from the age of fifteen, her rise to stardom on stage and on screen was meteoric. Within two years she was playing Ophelia at Stratford opposite Robert Helpmann and Paul Scofield, and she was still only twenty when Charlie Chaplin cast her, in 1952, to star as the dancer in his magical film *Limelight*. The same year that *Limelight* was premiered in London, Claire Bloom was performing at the Old Vic, where Kenneth Tynan described her as the best Juliet he had ever seen. Since then she has enjoyed a distinguished acting career in Hollywood, New York and London. Her many stage and screen successes include *Richard III* with Laurence Olivier, *Look Back in Anger* with Richard Burton, and *A Doll's House* with Ralph Richardson. Her portrayal of Blanche du Bois in *A Streetcar Named Desire* won the three major London dramatic awards in 1974. More recently she has played Gertrude in the BBC Television production of *Hamlet* and Lady Marchmain in Granada Television's acclaimed production of Evelyn Waugh's *Brideshead Revisited*.

Claire Bloom

★☆★☆★☆★☆★☆★☆★☆

LIMELIGHT
AND AFTER

The Education of an Actress

PENGUIN BOOKS

For my mother and my brother,
and for Anna and Philip

Penguin Books Ltd, Harmondsworth, Middlesex, England
Penguin Books, 40 West 23rd Street, New York, New York 10010, U.S.A.
Penguin Books Australia Ltd, Ringwood, Victoria, Australia
Penguin Books Canada Ltd, 2801 John Street, Markham, Ontario, Canada L3R 1B4
Penguin Books (N.Z.) Ltd, 182-190 Wairau Road, Auckland 10, New Zealand

First published in the United States of America by
Harper & Row, Publishers, Inc., 1982
First published in Canada by Fitzhenry & Whiteside Limited 1982
First published in Great Britain by Weidenfeld and Nicolson 1982
Published in Penguin Books in the United States of America by
arrangement with Harper & Row, Publishers, Inc.
Published in Penguin Books 1983

Made and printed in Great Britain by
Richard Clay (The Chaucer Press) Ltd,
Bungay, Suffolk
Set in Palatino

Contents

Illustrations

☆1☆
LIMELIGHT

Rooting and Uprooting

I was born in North Finchley, a suburb of London, on February 15, 1931, the daughter of Edward Bloom and his wife, Elizabeth Grew. They were the children of Jewish parents, and among the first generation in either family to be born in England, my father in Liverpool, my mother in London.

My father's father came from somewhere in Russia, his wife, Caroline, from Riga, in Russian Latvia. He had died long before I was born and I know nothing of his life save that he was supposed to have loved music and played the violin. His vocation, presuming he had one, seems to have been as much a mystery to his children as later my own father's was to me. He couldn't have been much more than sixty when he died. Somehow he and my grandmother had managed to make their way from Eastern Europe as far as Germany, where my grandfather stole a passport bearing the family name that is still mine. Then they passed on with the tide of Jews bound for America, though themselves came to rest in Liverpool, the port from which they would have sailed west. There my father was born, one of four boys and three girls. My grandmother Caroline I found very remote and in no way do I remember her inspiring my affection. She was a stocky woman with cold blue eyes whom I can only seem to remember wrapped in a black Persian lamb coat. In some way my father's family seemed in shadow to me always, my mother's in light. My mother's mother, Pauline, born in German Alsace-Lorraine, was also a small woman, but finely made and totally feminine in bearing. Neither her features nor her colouring were notable and she had thin mousy hair whose texture I have inherited. But her pale grey eyes and her charm were considerable attributes, and she could look prettier in a hat, and draw more admiring glances, than many more beautiful women. One hat that she wore I still remember: soft brown with a veil, and mauve pansies around the brim. She had tiny feet, of which she was proud, and always bought her shoes at an expensive French shoe shop on Bond Street. My mother says that when Pauline was a young woman, her skin was the colour of pearls. Her knowledge of German poetry was astounding and she had a long quotation for every occasion, either from Goethe or from Schiller. She loved the theatre, and was apt to make comments on the proceedings in a loud voice. We saw *An Ideal Husband* together when I was about thirteen. When a fairly well-built actress declared herself to be dying of love, my grandmother said scathingly, and with volume, "Poor ting." She came to all my first nights but happily saved her comments about me for later.

Both she and my grandfather, Henry Grew, spoke

English with a strong accent, my grandfather's Russian, my grandmother's German. My grandfather, a formidable figure—and not merely in my eyes—was called "The Guv'nor" by his six sons, had a large handlebar moustache, but otherwise looked remarkably like late photographs of Leon Trotsky. By the time I was born the Grews had a flourishing furniture factory in London's East End and lived in Cricklewood, a mainly Jewish suburb in North London.

My grandmother Grew, the only one of the family in England who continued to practice Judaism, always gathered together as many of her family as possible on Friday night, the Sabbath eve. I don't remember the menu varying: chopped fish, chicken soup, roast chicken, and vermicelli pudding. Her father, whose memory she worshipped, had been the grand rabbi of Frankfurt, and his wife had made wigs for the orthodox Jewish women, who shaved their heads upon marrying. I believe my grandparents' marriage was an arranged one, and that my grandmother had been in love with a young doctor in Germany. My grandmother was in awe of my grandfather, and probably because of the profound dominance of *her* father and the low esteem in which women seem to have been held in her orthodox household, was nervous and frightened of men generally. I still remember—with fury, I must say—the "boys" being served dinner first on Friday nights while the women waited their turn. All this extreme female submissiveness came to play a part in forming my own mother's character, her strange mixture of brave independence and the most crushing timidity.

My grandfather Grew moved to England soon after

his marriage, at about the turn of the century, to see if he could build a future there. The sight of the drunks lying in the streets of post-Dickensian London so disgusted him, however, that he fled back to Germany almost immediately. I have no idea what caused him to try again, but he must have returned not long afterwards with my grandmother, and they started married life together in a working-class district in the North of London. There the first three of their nine children were born. My mother was the third. My grandfather had opened a workshop, making small wooden picture frames and other objects then termed "fancy goods." In time, because of his success, he was able to start a furniture factory specialising in wooden mouldings, and the family moved to North London to a house that had a ballroom and a conservatory. In that house my mother spent her girlhood and from there she was married.

She met my father soon after she returned from New York. She had gone to America as a secretary, following across the Atlantic a married American man for whom she had worked in London, and with whom she had fallen in love, as he with her. But after two lonely and tormented years, she decided to return home. The respectable middle-class young men who had taken her out before she had left England no longer called, for my mother's adventure was known, and she was considered a "loose woman." Photographs of her at that time show a dark-eyed young woman, with wide, high cheekbones, and an expression combining a certain amount of melancholy with a lot of determination. Though not in any way pretty, she was strikingly handsome, with the gypsyish good looks that she has never lost. She found my father bright and amusing but I don't think she fell in love. For one thing, my mother believed that could never happen more than once, a belief she passed on to me and which I held for far too long. My father had little to offer: no savings, a modest job, small prospects. I think she felt that she could mould him, "make something out of him," and she had wanted always to marry and have a large family. He was a slight, black-haired man, not much taller than she, and spoke with a Liverpool accent. His saving grace was his sense of humour, but the unfortunate truth about him was revealed in his weak mouth. He was four years younger than my mother, and in reality, younger even than that. They married— my mother wearing a dress of green velvet with a silver lace veil—and went off to Paris for their honeymoon. Then back to London to start life in a tiny flat, with some financial help from her father, some silver-painted furniture from the "business," and little else. It has always been hard for me to say what my father did for a living. My birth certificate describes him as a salesman and so he was from time to time. He also managed from time to time to go into business for himself, early on with a partner in a tie business which quickly went bankrupt. My mother must have seen very soon all that his charm had at first concealed, but by then she was expecting her first child.

I occasionally pass the block of flats where I was born. It stands on a corner of the Finchley Road and Child's Hill, a short walk from Hampstead Heath. A large, timbered edifice in what is known as "Mock Tudor," looking like Anne Hathaway's cottage gone wild and distinguished only by a plaque, which records that W. G. Grace, the great cricketer, had once lived there. I was born at home, weighing five pounds but so round and plump, I am told, that the nurse put me back on the scale twice to make sure she wasn't mistaken. When I was nearly four, we moved from Finchley to Ruislip, still a suburb of London, but at that time much greener and almost rural. I remember no more from these first years than most people do: crawling after my mother, the hem of her dress, her feet, a doll I had. Most clearly I remember following my mother, following her everywhere, never leaving her alone. My father doesn't seem to exist for me, perhaps because he was away from home so much on "business." My friends were children of my mother's cousin, about my age, who lived in a house nearby, and had a sandbox. A sense of great security and well-being attaches to these memories, yet I know now that we were living close to disaster most of the time. However, my parents never quarrelled in front of me, not in these earliest years, and nothing led me to think anything was wrong. The flat was sunny and pleasant, and the silver furniture in my parents' bedroom was always there, even when everything else began to go to pay my father's debts. My father had some kind of a job, but my grandfather had still to help us out with money, especially as the expenses began to grow at about the time my brother John was to be born.

I had no idea that another child was expected. I was told only that I was to be sent away for a few days, to stay with my Aunt Mary, who had a daughter, Norma, a little older than I. By our standards they were very rich and lived in a house in Charles Street, in Mayfair. I went, very unhappy, to stay there, for I hated to leave my mother.

My mother's sister, Mary Grew, who was to play an important part in my life, was at that time a leading actress in London's West End. She was the wife of a producer named Victor Sheridan, whom I remember as small, elegant, and unfriendly, and whom she divorced after twenty years of marriage. Mary was one of the brilliant people I have known, and I often have wondered if her gifts didn't lie outside the theatre, in the struggle for women's rights. She performed in *The Combined Maze* by Frank Vosper in 1927, and the next year played in *Justice* and *Loyalties*, both by Galsworthy. She played Regina in *Ghosts* and Laura in *The Father*. In 1930 she had a great success in Elmer Rice's *Street Scene*. I never saw her at her best, for after performing the harrowing role of a woman about to be executed for the murder of her husband in *The Adding Machine* in the early thirties, she suffered a severe nervous breakdown, developing a skin disease which left her a semi-invalid and all but terminated her career as an actress.

I never realised, until I read her obituary in the *Times* in 1973, how alike our aims as actresses were. Although Mary never joined the Old Vic or played at Stratford, as I was to do, we believed in common that the theatre was a place of *importance*. Her career seems to have been shaped by choices similar to my own. Both of us were decidedly, even painfully, serious, and neither of us ever played in a good comedy. Mary's ambition, frustrated by her illness, was to play Hedda Gabler. When I opened in a preview of *A Doll's House* in New York several years before her death, she sent me this letter. (I was to open in *Hedda Gabler* shortly afterward and play the two Ibsen plays in repertory.)

Dec. 31, 1970

Dearest Claire,

This is to wish you a happy and successful New Year. I hear the preview went marvellously and I know it will be a great success, for it has come in the time of your life when you can give it its full meaning. And so has Hedda. I want to quote you a line from a new book by Melvyn Bragg called *The Hired Man,* which has won the PEN book prize for 1970. It expresses the frustrated lives of the agricultural community from 1890 to the end of the First World War, and has this sentence—

"War is the way men revenge the sacrifice of their cheated instincts."

This sums up Hedda. Her creative instincts are frustrated by the false values of the society she lives in and by her own cowardice in not breaking through them. Creative instincts which are prevented from expression revenge themselves in destruction. This is man's history and Hedda's.

I always wanted to play Hedda, so do it for me.

All my love and best wishes,

Mary

Mary lived the life of an actress in the grand, glamourous, old style of pre-war London. She was dressed exquisitely by the House of Worth and always had the air of a "star." My cousin Norma and the governess seemed quite cut off from the main household, ate their meals separately, walked gloomily in Kensington Gardens, and if Mary was working, only saw her at teatime, before she went to the theatre. As Mary was tiny and pretty, and Victor was neither, they were called, behind their backs, Beauty and the Beast. Dinner was taken at the Ritz or the Savoy, rarely at home.

After my home, where everything was easy-going, if slightly disordered, Mary's seemed to me horribly constrained. I stayed in the children's part of the house, where Norma and I shared a room. I was taken to see Mary when I arrived, shown to her as she lay on her settee, and removed almost at once. All would have been well if Norma and I had got on better together, but back then we didn't. She thought me a baby, I thought her a snob. I cried to go home most of the time. I was away from my mother only five days, but I remember clearly those first strong fears of rejection which have troubled me always. I didn't understand why I had been sent away, although I realized something was happening from which I was being deliberately shut out. I had always felt until then that I shared everything with my mother. I was overjoyed when I was told I could go home, but when I got there my mother was in bed. I thought she must be ill. Then the nurse who was with her showed me a cot, with a tiny, and I thought hideous, baby in it. No one had told me another child was going to live in my house. I was shocked and started to cry. I hid in a cupboard and wouldn't speak to anyone all day. I came to accept the baby eventually, though it took me years to love my brother John as I do now.

One of my pleasures since childhood has been to walk in the country and pick the wild flowers. There was not much open country near our house in Ruislip, but I had an aunt and uncle who lived in Hampshire, not far from the sea. So when we went to visit, I had the added joy of walking on the cliffs and gathering the sweet scented pinks that grew there and smelled of cloves. Near the cottage was a disused gravel pit, in high summer full of wild strawberries I picked and brought home to my mother for our dessert. The meadows were full of cowslips, primroses, and wild daisies, and the marshy fields of great blue iris.

This uncle and aunt had two children roughly our age, Erica and Michael. Erica was wiry and full of energy, and I was envious of her black curly hair and of her fearlessness about—so it seemed to me, so full of fears—*everything*. She could chatter on charmingly for hours about nothing in particular and I thought her pretty and myself plain. Without question I was sexually jealous of the attraction this outgoing little girl seemed to hold for my father, and throughout my life have always felt at a loss beside her kind of vivacity in other women.

Shortly after my brother John was born, we moved again, this time to Cardiff. As my father had immense charm, was possessed, as everyone said, of "a wonderful sense of humour," but had no sense of responsibility at all, we were in fact always moving.

I don't think I've ever minded that because of all this moving, I had little formal schooling worth anything. I was clearly never cut out to be an academic student; nonetheless, the rootlessness did bewilder me and nourished my fearfulness and my melancholy side. I made no lasting friendships and hardly any even of a transitory nature. Neither did my mother, who came increasingly to rely on parents, sisters, cousins, and on me. This brought us closer than an ordinary mother and daughter, but placed a strain on me of which I was not to be fully conscious for years. I never wanted my mother to feel lonely and so, despite her urging me to go out and to make friends— contrary, of course, to her own example—I would stay at home with her. I grew from a child always asking to be read to, to one who always read. I read everything I could, from Charles Kingsley's *The Water Babies* to *Jane Eyre.* I had no idea of the literary value or the cultural status of these books—I just opened them and disappeared. Oliver Twist was a companion, as was David Copperfield. I admired Jo in *Little Women,* but with Beth I was one. What was it I disappeared *from?* The dark. The hand that would emerge from under the bed to catch my legs as I was to climb in under the sheet. The cupboard that led to another cupboard, and yet another, and in which I would be lost, in which I would vanish when I went to get my coat. The bath that was not really a bath, but, if I shut my eyes, the sea in which I would drown. I disappeared for a time from my fears, and I was afraid of nearly everything.

School. I remember being taken by my mother to school in Cardiff for the first time—my feeling of doom not unlike a first night—and I remember the relief when she came to pick me up. The only other thing I remember is being told how to tie my shoelaces, a lesson I resented, since I could already do this myself. I remember nothing else in between. Probably nothing else ever seemed so important to me as my mother's two appearances.

We were joined at home in Cardiff by an English girl from the West Country, called Rose, who was what was known in those days as a "mother's help." She was in her early twenties and she became my first true friend. She joined me in my earliest games of make-believe and enjoyed them as much as I did. For me they were as satisfying as walking in the fields, as reading Charles Dickens and the Brontës, and as being with my mother.

I don't know for sure if my father lost his job, but soon we were ready to move again, this time to Bristol. To cross over the Severn River then meant a ferry boat journey in your car for about twenty minutes. Nothing to worry about. But when we arrived, the river was raging like a rough sea and we were told that we were just in time, the last ferry to go over before the Severn *bore,* a great rising tide that caused a huge and rapidly moving wave to sweep down the river. We went on board, and midway through the crossing the great wave washed over the boat and rushed in through the car doors, drenching us all. It was one of my greatest fears come true.

In Bristol we found a pleasant house on a hill, with a charming garden. By this time we had acquired a dog, a pair of tortoises, two parakeets, a white rabbit with a black stripe down its back, and some mice. The tortoises tunnelled their way out of our garden, the parakeets escaped from their cage, the mice were drowned in a great rainstorm that flooded their cage during the night, and a cat killed the rabbit. Only the dog, Topsy, survived.

I was sent to a different sort of school now, a very proper and correct one called Badminton, near to our house, and I would think, quite expensive. It was a boarding school but I was sent as a day pupil. We wore the usual gym slips—making us all look uniformly like lumps—white blouses and school ties, although our speech-day dresses, made of pale blue silk, were rather pretty. To be a day student in a school composed mainly of boarders put one at a disadvantage, as the groups of girls who were to spend whole terms together formed themselves quickly into exclusive cliques. Even so, I managed to make a friend or two, though the girl I secretly admired and whose name I still remember—Zanne Welch—didn't give me any attention at all.

The formidable headmistress, who wore her hair in a tight little bun, was Miss Baker. Each morning we would assemble to kneel on the hard floor for prayers. Next, the girls who had done something wrong were called out in front of the school to be reprimanded or punished. I always expected to hear my own name called, though for what crime I expected to be punished, I did not know.

Then one day I *was* called out of the room by one of the teachers. In the hallway she looked at me most dramatically and asked in a severe tone if I had something to tell her. I had no idea of what she was talking about and stood tongue-tied. Had I ever wanted to steal a pencil? she asked. I responded by twisting my hair in knots and trying to eat it. Then I went scarlet and started to cry. This she interpreted as a confession of guilt. We went back into the classroom where she told the other girls that I was in disgrace and was to be "put into coventry" for three days, meaning that no one was to speak to me for that time, nor I to them. She then showed me The Pencil, which I can still describe: white with blue and red stripes going around it, and impressed with the letters *R.A.F.* As I was always forgetting pencils and having to use someone else's, I had probably borrowed it. The charge

against me was that in the hearing of witnesses I had
said I wished to keep it and then had not given it back.
At any rate, it had been found on my desk and my fate
was sealed. I was too ashamed to tell my mother, and
let the three days of ostracism pass without a word. But
at the end of that time I had a new friend and ally, Zanne
Welch. Like all the popular girls, she was terrific at gym
and sports and so were all her friends. When, to my mortification, I had become an outcast, she had taken notice
of me for the first time, and she and her friends became
my protectors and "took me up"—partly out of kindness
and partly in defiance of the school. So I became one of
a group I had admired, the "fast group," the girls with
"spirit." To add to my sense that I was all at once on
the up-and-up, I was chosen to play the princess in *Rumpel-
stiltskin* who spins straw into gold. With this I felt more
than "accepted" or "included"—I felt important. I felt the
joy of pretending to be someone else and saw how with
it every trace of shyness vanished. It was a feeling of
rightness, akin to what I had experienced when I first discovered reading.

It must have been about then that I was taken to
the film of *Romeo and Juliet.* I had been seven when my
mother had first read this play to me—and *Hamlet* and *A
Midsummer Night's Dream*—while we were sitting in the sun
in the garden of my uncle's house in Milford. I had loved
the sound of the words and was fascinated by what
rhymed, but had only the vaguest idea of what was going
on or what it meant. In the film, Juliet was played by
Norma Shearer, Romeo by Leslie Howard. They were both
too old for their roles, and the production would seem

old-fashioned today, but to me it revealed a world of passion and romantic love for the first time—of lovers parted and united in death, of hopeless despair and indescribable joy. I went home to act out the balcony scene over and over. I went to a fancy dress party complete with a "Juliet cap."

At about this time, Rose, my dearest companion, left to go home and take care of her father. I thought I would never get over the loss. In a day, such being the way with small children, I completely recovered, and we were joined at home by another young woman, Kathleen Jones, from a small town in Wales. Kathleen was even more devoted to "let's pretend" than Rose and into the bargain was able to sew costumes, and once more I had a partner for my theatrical games. With my parents and my brother as captive audience, we gave potted versions of Shakespeare, of fairy stories, and of girls' adventure books. I played the lead.

In spite of my new eminence at school, I lived for the holidays, when we always seemed to be able to go to lovely places. The first summer in Bristol we went to a Devonshire fishing village called Beer, and took two rooms in a cottage facing the sea. The great thrill for me was to go out deep-sea fishing. We left at five in the morning, after a strong cup of tea, and sailed off to find the mackerel to bring home for breakfast. The most popular boat was owned by a Captain Ralph, and it was with him I longed to go because he was remarkably handsome. I don't remember my father being with us. Where was he? I don't know.

The next summer we went to stay at a cottage in

Cornwall, near a point in the coast named Bedruthen Steps—a stretch of beach that had been used by eighteenth-century smugglers who were transporting rum and, as we liked to believe, burying gold. The magnificent beaches were full of hidden coves and in the rocks pools of water deep enough to swim in. We climbed the smaller cliffs looking for gulls' eggs and hidden treasure, and, as I remember, John and I were always hungry, and looking forward to our tea with scones and strawberry jam and thick Cornish cream, which we ate in a café high up on the cliffs overlooking the sea.

One day during the last week of our holiday, the radio was playing loudly when we went for our morning tea and everyone seemed sad as they listened. I was a child full of the joy of the beach and couldn't understand why anyone would be feeling unhappy on a bright summer day. I never connected the thought of war with the mood that pervaded the tearoom. I must have heard war spoken of and I had seen frightening newsreels of children being bombed in China, but I was eight years old, safe on a holiday with the people I most loved, and unprepared for what I heard.

The radio music was interrupted by a voice announcing the Prime Minister, Neville Chamberlain. He spoke slowly and sounded tired. ". . . His Majesty's government has received no such communication or assurance. I must therefore tell you that a state of war . . ." We were at war. Someone near us started to cry. I cried too, my mouth full of scones and jam. We didn't know what to do or where to go. John kept asking what was wrong. I still didn't know what it meant, I just felt cold and afraid.

We wandered out into the bright afternoon, making our way back to the cottage, while an air-raid alarm sounded—as it did in many places in England that day. It was a false alarm, but we didn't know that. As there was no house in sight, we took shelter under some trees at the side of the road. Soon after, the all-clear sounded, one long clear note. Nothing quite yet had happened to England or to us.

My mother decided that as our holiday was nearly over anyway, it would be better to go home and be all together, so back we went to Bristol. There was no feeling there that anything had changed; still vacation time, a beautiful summer. The crisis that came hadn't to do with the war but with my father and his finances, which necessitated that we sell the house and that I be taken out of Badminton School. My mother, brother, and I were now to go back to Cornwall where we would rent a cottage, and John and I would go to the village school. I was told that we would be safer there, as our house in Bristol stood on a hill and was exposed to enemy aircraft. Actually, we had to leave because we were broke, and school in the Cornwall village would be free and the living fairly cheap.

I was delighted to leave Badminton, for though I had come to terms with the snobbishness of the girls and the righteousness of the teachers, I had never liked it there. My real sorrow was in saying goodbye to my acting partner and friend, Kathleen, who went home to Wales. This time it took me more than the day I had spent grieving over Rose when she'd left.

My father went off to Hampshire, where his brother

had a house, to see if he could find a job and a permanent place for us to live, and we took the train back to Cornwall. My mother had written to arrange a place for us to rent, so we moved, sight unseen, into a tiny cottage much more primitive than our last one. The unhappiness all this caused my mother I could not fully understand at the time. I knew that she had wept when we left the Bristol house and I had hardly ever seen her weep before, but the adventure of a new life took hold of me completely, particularly crossing the garden at night to reach the outdoor privy. Instead of electric lights we had paraffin lamps, whose oily odour I liked to smell, and our source of water in the garden was a well that had to be pumped by hand. John, who was now four, was entered along with me in the village school, about three miles' walk from our house. Students of all sizes and ages took their lessons in one big room, with a female teacher for the younger children like John, and a male teacher, referred to as "Sir," for the older group where I was placed. The village school was a big change from the stuffiness of Badminton—informal, unruly, and brutal in punishing the disobedient. For the first time I saw boys being caned and heard them howl from the pain.

Nothing about the war seemed to touch us there. We had no radio and I don't remember seeing a newspaper. It was beautiful and still in the Cornish village, and the fiercest moment that I can remember from the autumn of 1939 was a visit by a large pig who had escaped his pen and run wild in our front garden.

In October, my father came to say he had settled us in the small town of New Milton, near Milford, where I had already spent happy summers. I was disappointed to be moving again and all that cheered me up was that New Milton was near to the country. It was pouring when we arrived. The garden consisted of mud and an unfinished rock garden of extreme horror. The house was barely even a bungalow, and though I didn't mind it terribly, it was another disappointment to my mother after life in Bristol.

So, I was entered in another school—my fourth—Fern Hill Manor, where my cousin Erica already attended. Here, in a large nineteenth-century house set on the edge of town, the educational methods fell somewhere between the eighteenth-century eccentricity of the Cornish village school and the strict regimentation of Badminton. This may have suited me, for I did well scholastically and even won third prize for running.

That Christmas John and I were taken to see *Where the Rainbow Ends,* a play for children about St. George and the Dragon. It was the first real play—as opposed to pantomime—that I had seen and, as it was revived from year to year, probably the first play to be seen by many children of my generation. St. George disappearing magnificently amid clouds of smoke and claps of thunder made his impression, and though I can't say it was my turning point— the film of *Romeo and Juliet* had been that—I could not forget those marvellous transformations on a stage.

We soon found that New Milton was no haven from the war. The bombing started in earnest, both day and night, only stopping for some reason at three in the morning, when we would finally hear the planes fade away. After a few weeks we learned to distinguish between the sounds of a German and an English plane. The German engines had a short, repeating pattern, while ours had a long-drawn-out hum. On our location near the coast, the German planes chose to unload what was left of their cargo of bombs instead of going on and wasting them at sea. From one direction we got the bombs they hadn't had time to drop on London and from the other the bombs they hadn't dropped on Southampton. They even machine-gunned our main street. I remember the uproar when a spy dressed as a nun was discovered (supposedly) signalling from the water tower. Spies in equally blasphemous attire were said to have been seen in a number of villages like ours.

Finally things got too bad for Fern Hill Manor to remain open. Most of the students were sent off to boarding schools in a safer part of the country, and my cousin, Erica, went with them.

My aunt in Milford was an invalid confined to a wheel chair, and my uncle decided he must take her away to a place where she could get some sleep at night. He offered to let us stay in their house, which had an air-raid shelter. This meant we could go to sleep in the shelter at night instead of getting out of bed and cowering in the corridors of the house whenever the siren sounded. It seemed another good idea, so we moved ourselves and our things yet again.

We arrived, unpacked—and the church bells rang. It was 1940 and France had already fallen. Throughout the war the bells were only to ring to signal an invasion. My mother went silently upstairs and put on her fur coat. We sat all together in the living room. My parents had no illusions about what would befall a Jewish family when the Germans came, even though we did not yet know the full facts of what was happening in Europe. So we sat there, waiting, until the police came around to tell us that it had been a false alarm. I hardly remember what my father did in the face of this trial—I only remember my mother waiting in her best coat to meet the Germans.

The next few nights were peaceful and there was a cozy kind of fun even in taking tea and biscuits out to the end of the garden where we all snugly slept in our own bunks. Apart from my fear that we would be buried alive, I quite enjoyed it. But on the third night, after we had settled down to sleep, the shelter suddenly rose from the ground—or so it felt—and dropped again with a thud. Explosions louder by far than anything we had heard before sounded around us. Even after quiet came again, we stayed in the shelter until dawn, afraid to go out to see what had happened. At daybreak, we heard the voice of the warden calling, "Is everyone all right in there?" We answered shakily that we were, and my father went out to ask him what had happened.

The warden told him that "land mines," much larger and more powerful than ordinary aerial bombs, had been dropped in a circle around us. My father and I went out in the early light to have a look at the craters that marked the nearby fields. As we walked back in silence, stunned by the thought of our narrow escape, there was a large explosion that sent us running for home. The police arrived and said the area was to be cleared because there were time bombs everywhere. My parents decided, Blitz or no Blitz, to leave for my grandparents' house in London. By now we had nowhere else to go.

In London everything was in confusion and we didn't know how long we would be able to stay. The Grews' large house was crammed with uncles in the army, navy and air force who came and went on leave, and my mother's youngest sister, Marguerite, recently separated from her husband, was living there with her young daughter. And the Blitz was reaching its height. Of my grandmother's London house I remember mostly the underside of the kitchen table. I hadn't time for anything else to make an impression, for within only weeks I was again on the move.

John and I were now sent to join my cousin Norma in the country at a school run by Dora Russell, a former wife of Bertrand Russell's, whose ideas on progressive education she was trying to put into practice. No one, including the teachers, had to wear clothes unless he wanted to. No one had to attend class unless he wanted to. Everyone was to be free to do as he or she wished. As I remember it, no one did much of anything. After the initial shock of seeing male teachers nude, I got into the mood of the place and discovered how delightful it was to swim naked and to be at a school where I hadn't any schoolwork. We spent hours in the dormitories at night talking about sex, and though the point of the Russell school was to make us free spirits, I believe we were the smuttiest-minded group of little children in England. Although all the facts of life I learned from my friends turned out invariably to be off the mark, I found this school, which bore no resemblance to a school, much to my liking. That is, for the three weeks that I was there.

For now an invitation had come from my father's

brother, who lived in Florida, saying that if we would wish to, we might stay with his family in America for the duration of the war. Because my grandfather couldn't go on supporting the whole family indefinitely, my mother had decided that it would be best to take us out of the country. Florida must have seemed to her the only, if not the last, way out of our interminable and wearing sojourns. I believe, though, that once the transatlantic move had been set in motion she bitterly regretted it. However, my father had run out of money again and that, no less than the war, accounted for her decision. She didn't know which way to turn, except to something uncertain and unknown.

John and I were brought home from school and told the news. I remember feeling enormous excitement at the idea of the spectacular journey. What it would be like to leave my father, our relatives, and my country to go off and live with total strangers for no one knew how long, I couldn't begin to grasp. I had the sense of importance a child feels to be doing something dramatic.

Despite the magnitude of the journey, there were few preparations to be made. We had no house to close up and few friends to say goodbye to.

My father accompanied us on the train to Glasgow. It was 1941; I was ten, John was nearly six. We were to sail from Glasgow in a convoy, on a ship that was evacuating children, either with their mothers or alone. The journey would take about ten days and began, as many things, large and small, do in Britain, on a cold, grey, wet day. Not until I saw the ship did I understand what we were doing—and that we couldn't turn back—and then I was all at once full of terror. I had never seen a man cry until my father, in tears, came on deck carrying in his hand a packet of biscuits he had just bought. Everyone who wasn't travelling was told to leave and we went down to our cabin, where we sat and waited for the boat to move off. Despite the presence of John and my mother, I cannot remember having felt so solitary and abandoned ever before. It was the last moment of something, probably of my childhood. What happened after that happened to the person that I recognise as myself.

2

Innocence Abroad

To avoid the U-boats, the ship cut a swerving course. During the day we had life-boat drills and at night went to bed with our clothes on, dressed for disaster. The smell of oil seemed to be everywhere. The food tasted of little else. Occasionally some kind passenger would organise a diversion for the children, a quiz or a talent contest, but I remember the journey as frightening, tedious, and endless. On our eighth day the captain announced that we were in safe waters and would dock three days later in New York harbour. I was suddenly in a great state of excitement—another great state of excitement—and never thought for a moment about the realities of our situation, and John was too young to understand. But my mother understood only too well. The English families that chose to go abroad were not allowed to take any money beyond the barest minimum, and once in the States we were to be totally dependent upon our relations. They had offered to take into their midst a family who'd had little sense of security to begin with, and now had virtually none:

in charge, a mother highly nervous with strangers and unable to assert herself among more dominating natures; with her, a ten-year-old daughter full of her own, largely uninformed, opinions, and intolerant of anyone whose intelligence she judged to be less developed than her own; and a little boy, needy and frightened.

The famous New York skyline was spectacular—terrifyingly so. To me, the Statue of Liberty looked more menacing than anything else, her torch raised as though to bring it down and crush any boat that passed beneath. Nor was I alone in my feelings of apprehension and helplessness.

The immigration authorities came on board and we had to see them in the ship's main dining room. To go through the passenger list took them nearly all day. Every family had to be interviewed about their political views— we ourselves didn't claim any—and then about their financial prospects, ours none too promising. I knew about Ellis Island from a Chaplin film, and when I heard us described by the officials as "refugees," I was sure we would end up there for good. However, toward evening we were given visas, and made our way down the gangplank. To be locked away on Ellis Island seemed, all at once, preferable to coming ashore in the dark into a great, unknown city.

Our aunt in Fort Lauderdale, Florida, had sent one of her cousins to meet us. She lived nearby, in New Rochelle, and we stayed with her three days to recover from the anxiety of the voyage (and from the swaying of the ship). Then, by Greyhound bus, we started our three-day journey to Florida. We travelled day and night, supposedly sleeping in our seats. I loved the nights. Wide awake, I sat up covered with a blanket and waited for the next stop, where we would get off at something marvellous called a "drugstore," there to drink hot milk and to eat warm and fragrant cinnamon doughnuts. We lived on milk and doughnuts for most of the journey, as my mother wanted to hold on to the little money we had.

When the landscape began to grow tropical, I looked through the bus window for crocodiles and Africans. I saw palm trees and cactus and cotton fields, but nothing to approach the exoticism of the drugstore.

About our disastrous stay in Florida with my aunt and uncle and their two children, I will say little. Forty years have passed, but I am still reluctant to hurt people who were kind to us in their way. Then too, so much that was bad there, I have deliberately forgotten over the years. My aunt and uncle were extremely conservative and conventional in their outlook. We were two families who should never have been thrown together, but as they say, there was a war on. We had been there almost a year when John was given a watch by my aunt and uncle as a Christmas present. John was lonely and bored and he traded it with another little boy in the neighbourhood for the excitement of some tin soldiers. He wasn't quite seven. The boy's parents felt they should report this criminal propensity to my uncle, who berated John furiously over dinner. My mother asked him to leave the boy alone: he was still a baby, and, as she went off every day to work in my uncle's dress shop, a neglected one at that. My uncle pushed my mother out of the way and raised his hand as though to strike her. Terrified, I tried to get between them. "Don't you dare touch my mother!" I screamed, at which he hit me hard on both sides of my face. A few months later we left on the Greyhound bus for the trip north.

All I remember with pleasure of the year in Florida was the dancing school in Fort Lauderdale where I went after school each day to study ballet, tap, and musical comedy dancing, which consisted largely of doing hand-stands and cartwheels. I was recruited for the school by a teacher called Betty Boxer, who with her husband, Irving Plumber, had read in the local newspaper about our arrival, and then happened to hear me sing on the radio. I had entered and won a radio quiz contest and talent competition for children my age. My radio appearance had made me a minor celebrity at my school, to the disgruntlement of my cousins, whom I was always criticising, and one day my mother was telephoned by the British War Relief and asked if I would entertain at benefits to raise money for England. In the following weeks I sang each night at another big Miami hotel, including one that bore the star-tling sign on its door, "Gentiles Only." I was put to sleep at eight each evening like all other schoolchildren, but then at eleven was awakened, sleepily got into my party clothes, and was driven off in a limousine with my mother to another hotel. Thus I broke into show business, singing, with no small amount of pathos, a little song, written especially for me by Irving Plumber of the Fort Lauderdale dancing school:

> I'm a little English girl,
> Knocking at your door,
> Driven from my home,
> By the Gods of War,

Asking but the right,
To live and share the sun,
Praying for the night,
When peace once more will come.

Before we left Florida, my mother had begun to in-
quire if there was any way to get us home. Whatever
might be happening to England she wanted to share with
the people she loved. But all she could manage was for
us to escape Florida for the north. My mother wrote to
her London cousin, Lily, who had gone to live with her
brother in Forest Hills, New York. There, on 113th Street,
Lily found us a cheap room, assuring my mother that she
could earn enough for our food and rent by taking baby-
sitting jobs. It was a two-story house on a dreary street.
In the room there was a double bed for mother and me,
a single for John, an armchair that had once been stuffed,
a table, and a radio. The radio was to be at the center
of our life for the next eighteen months: our source of
entertainment and our source of war news. We shared a
bathroom and my mother shared the kitchen with Mrs.
Alma Jorgenson, the woman from whom our room was
rented, a rather beautiful widow of Swedish descent, who
lived in the house with her own mother and two children.
John and I enrolled in school—yet another school—and
my mother was given the names of people for whom she
might be able to baby sit. We settled down to wait out
the war.

At least we felt free, if still not that secure. The Jorgensons were like us in temperament—not too particular about
meals or household schedules—and the daughter, Virginia,
and I became fellow dreamers instantly. She wanted to

become a model and marry a rich man (she subsequently did both) and I wanted to be an actress. We spent hours talking about how beautiful life was going to be when we grew up; how beautiful *we* would be. As I was skinny, with thin hair and large teeth, the possibility seemed more remote for me than for Virginia, who was tall for her age, with blue eyes and blond hair. We read *Screen Romances* and *Movie Life,* and when the money was found, rushed to the movie house on Continental Avenue to see wonderful South Sea Island films with Jon Hall and Dorothy Lamour—*Volcano, Tornado, Hurricane.* Hibiscus flowers and mountains of lava. Blue grottoes and mysterious idols. Total escape and immeasurable joy.

My mother joined a small private library close by across Queens Boulevard. It stayed open until midnight, and so as soon as you finished reading one book, you could run out and get another. I began to read everything, from *Sue Barton, District Nurse* to the Brontës and A. J. Cronin. I read Hardy's *Jude the Obscure,* sensing that the passion and the despair that drove Jude to his death was of a different order from what drove Jon Hall and Dorothy Lamour, but understanding little else. At night we read and listened to the radio: "Inner Sanctum," Fred Allen, Jack Benny, and most important of all, more crucial even than news of the war, "Your Hit Parade." I suppose I did school work, but not because it captured my imagination and not that I can remember doing it, either. The nights that my mother was out baby sitting, I woke up precisely at midnight to see if she had come in yet. I continued waking up at midnight for years and years, even after we were in England. I wanted to be home. So did my mother, and together we waited for something to happen. We were always waiting, for all that life had settled into a peaceful routine.

A letter arrived one day from a Wall Street bank. My father had sent us money, but we would have to come and get it. So the three of us dressed in our best, which wasn't too fine by this time, and off we went. We entered a tall office building and went up in the elevator to an imposing suite of offices. My mother was shown through an inner door, while John and I stayed in the waiting room. There was a large lamp beside me, with a map of the world on the shade. I remember looking on it for England. When mother came out she said, "Let's go for a walk." We walked along the Battery and rather shakily she told us—for she still couldn't believe it: "They have allowed Eddie to send us twenty pounds every month and he has asked the bank to try to book us on a Portuguese ship. From Portugal we can fly to England." We were all shaky by then. "And now," said my mother, "let's go and buy you some new clothes."

We went to Best's on Fifth Avenue. The outfit I got I remember in every detail: a blue and white suit of tiny checks with a pleated skirt, a white blouse, blue patent shoes, and a leghorn straw hat with a blue ribbon. I could see myself wearing it on the Portuguese ship.

But when summer came we were still in Forest Hills, and mother wasn't feeling well. Without telling us, she went for a hospital examination and when she came home took me for another of our long walks. I didn't know the word "cancer," but I knew something dreadful was imminent when she told me she would have to have an operation. We had to walk and walk and walk before it was possible for me to go home and pretend to John that everything was all right.

With mother going into hospital, no one knew what to do with us. Lily contacted the British War Relief, for whom I had entertained the guests in Florida, and within a week they had found a camp in Massachusetts, "Shari-lawn," that would take John and me for nothing. The week before we left I was sure that if we went to the camp I would never see my mother again. When we said goodbye at the bus depot, I felt the same dread I had when we had left my father behind and boarded the ship for America.

The first weeks at camp were overshadowed by loneli-ness and worry about my mother. John went off to the boys' camp, which was separate from the girls' facilities, and we hardly saw each other. The girls in my cabin were all sporty and well off, and, at twelve and thirteen, talked only of boys. I hadn't even been to the movies with a boy, other than John. They all had fluffy pink angora sweaters, the fashion that year. I longed for one, even while waiting to hear if my status was to be changed from refugee to orphan. Only when I received the news that mother's operation had been a success (the growth was found to be benign) did my love affair with Sharilawn begin—with the lake, with the campfires, with my copper ashtray and my leather belt, and with the theatre.

The project that summer was a Gilbert and Sullivan operetta, *Patience.* The larger parts were cast with the older girls, but I got a role as one of Patience's companions, with a little solo to sing. That was all I cared about from then on. When the performance night came, and most of the parents were arriving for the weekend, I was sad that my mother was still not strong enough to travel. But the thrill of getting into costume while an audience was gathering in the theatre made me forget even that. I wore a black dress made of tulle, and enough spangle to satisfy even me. And a lot of makeup. When I looked in the mirror at my blue eyeshadow and my bright red lipstick—an application that would have seen Carmen Miranda through a whole season—I thought I was beautiful.

We arrived home from the summer to be met by our mother at the bus terminal. She looked frail. She had been in our room for a month, trying to look after herself while she recovered from the surgery; we had been in the lovely countryside, swimming in the lake and being served in the dining room. It was an emotional reunion for an emotional family—especially as there was still no news of the Portuguese ship aboard which I would wear my blue and white check suit.

Because of the allowance my father was sending, there was now some pocket money for me, and I began to buy, on the instalment plan, Shakespeare's collected plays, in a red leather binding. For my twelfth birthday, mother got tickets for the theatre. We went to Broadway and saw *Junior Miss*. I realized that it wasn't Shakespeare, or even *Patience*, but I loved it. Then one Saturday she took us to see a second play, *The Three Sisters*, with Katharine Cornell, Judith Anderson, Ruth Gordon, and Edmund Gwenn.

From then on I thought only of going into the theatre and playing in Chekhov. *Junior Miss* was fun, Chekhov was *moving*. That's what I was looking for—something more moving even than my own plight as a little English girl driven from my home by the Gods of War. Chekhov and Katharine Cornell made all that seem like nothing.

About this time, as I was listening one morning to Robert Emory's "Rainbow Hour," a programme of radio plays for children, they announced an open audition for any child who wrote in and asked to be heard. I immediately wrote in and asked to be heard. I also answered a newspaper advertisement offering some lucky girl a scholarship at the Marie Moser School of Dancing in Manhattan, and arranged for my mother to take me to audition at their studios in Steinway Hall on West 57th Street. When we arrived, there were pretty girls everywhere, each looking to me utterly certain that the scholarship was hers. I went off with Miss Moser when my turn came and performed a little dance routine she gave me to do. I then sang a song and recited a poem and was awarded the scholarship on the spot, and told, moreover, that I had a bright future as a child model. I was shuffled off next door to have photographs taken of me at the school's expense. They were to act as my agents.

I had no sooner begun dancing classes twice a week at the Moser school when I was called to audition for Robert Emory. I got dressed in my Best's suit, with the picture hat, and got back on the subway for Manhattan, my mother at my side. At the radio station, I was led alone into a brightly lit and empty studio, where I stood in front of a microphone and was asked by a disembodied voice from the control room to tell everybody all about myself. I remember going on for a very long time, though what I had to tell everybody at such length I cannot imagine to this day. All I knew was that I was there and that, scared as I was, I shouldn't stop until somebody directed me to. Next an assistant came in and handed me a script. I was to read the role of Queen Elizabeth I of England (so apparently I had told them I was English). I read into the microphone in a Peg Leg Pete voice. I was trying to be at once blustery and regal, and that's what came out. "Thank you," said the disembodied voice; "please wait in the next room." Half an hour later I was told to return the next Saturday to play Queen Elizabeth in the morning play.

John came with my mother to watch my professional radio debut. I thought I would fall to pieces from shaking, and when I didn't, when in fact I began to enjoy enormously pretending to be a monarch over the airwaves, I thought the whole world must be listening to Robert Emory's "Rainbow Hour," and that no one out there would ever be the same again. As it happened, when we got home, I couldn't find anybody, apart from the Jorgensons, who had even heard me

I returned to being a school girl, except for my lessons at Marie Moser's. I loved everything about them: the studio's "show biz" atmosphere, the glamorous, pretty girls seething with vanity and ambition, the popular music playing as we practised, the 57th Street bustle down below the windows, and the Automat across the street where after class I ate hot chicken pie. Yes, I thought, this is surely "it." All I wanted was more. Most of the winter we rehearsed the song "For Me and My Gal," to be performed in the Central Park Mall in May. I was in the chorus. The day of the performance I dressed at home in frilly panties and full can-can costume, and then, pulling my bonnet onto my shoulder-length ringlets, once again boarded the subway for Manhattan. This time I thought that at the sight of me no one on the subway would ever be the same again. But you can fall over dead on the subway without making much impression on the passenger across the way. I arrived in Manhattan, my costume drenched from the mid-May heat, having yet to leave my mark on the world.

That summer John and I were invited back to Shari-lawn, where I played in the Humperdinck opera *Hansel and Gretel,* not in the chorus any longer, but as the star. I had nearly reached my full height that year, and though I was not then, or ever, much of a singer, I was a foot taller than the boy who played Hansel, and if nothing else, I left my mark on *him.* My mother was in the audience this time, her presence a great joy to me, especially as she had arrived at the camp with the news that we were booked onto a Portuguese ship sailing for Lisbon in the fall. There we would stay in a hotel that had been commandeered for evacuees, and wait our turn to be flown to England by the R.A.F.

We left America in 1943. No one came to see us off— for despite all my auditions and my lessons and my radio debut, we had still lived almost entirely to ourselves in our room, waiting for just this moment to arrive. There was almost a holiday spirit on board the freighter when we embarked. The ship was a neutral nation's—therefore safe from enemy torpedoes—and the passengers were mostly mothers with children. A German couple on board furnished most of the excitement. John and I were sure they were agents of the Gestapo (and had no trouble convincing the others our age). The food was gruesome and we were always hungry. We used to sit with the other children in the evening, watching the sun set into the wake of the ship, endlessly discussing the food. Horsemeat was served, not disguised in a stew or a pie, but flat out on your plate. Holding our noses against the sweetish scent and the horrible idea, we ate it. Then there was an October hurricane. Then news spread that the Germans claimed the Portuguese had violated their neutrality by allowing British ships to refuel at the Azores: Portugal would be in the war—and our ship a target for German attack—before the journey was out. So, in the end, we were as frightened coming as we had been going—seasick from the hurricane, revolted by the food, and certain to drown when the ship was sunk.

On the tenth day we landed in Lisbon and immediately were transferred to a train for Estoril, where we were put up in a lovely grand hotel, full of British families waiting their turn to go home. Many were returning because they had someone in England who was ill, or dying, and needed them. All were women and children. The only men in sight were the waiters. Every evening at about five, we were assembled in the grand salon to hear read out the names of those who would be leaving the next day. Families had been living there for months already. We knew we were in for a wait, and though we longed to go, we were all frightened of this last lap of the journey. Leslie Howard, the film actor, had been shot down a few days earlier on just such a flight as we were to make.

In the end we were there nearly three months. In that time I took up with a little band of English children who used to march around singing at the top of their voices the national anthems of all the Allied countries. We were very daring, since there were rumoured to be Nazi agents everywhere in Portugal, even behind the bushes in the lovely large gardens of our hotel.

In early January our names finally were read out in the grand salon. We didn't even have to pack. We had never unpacked. A bus came and we were driven to an airport. It was dark and the plane was heavily camouflaged. We were hustled off the bus and onto the plane. You could hardly see anything. It was so unreal as not even to be frightening. I didn't believe it was happening to me anyway. Eating hot chicken pie in the Automat across from Marie Moser's dancing school was what happened to me—not this. It wasn't until we were on board that I began to think about Leslie Howard.

The seats had been removed so as to take more passengers and the windows were blacked out. We were told to sit on the floor. There were ten passengers, two of them nuns. No one spoke. We just tried not to show each other our fear. One of the nuns was chewing gum. That was all I heard during the next five hours, apart from the hum of the engines. Then one of the crew, the first we had seen, put his head out of the cockpit door and said, "Hold on tight, we're going to land." When the doors were opened, the first fresh air came into the stuffy cabin. We had come down into the early dawn. We were just off shore somewhere. I didn't even know that we'd been on a seaplane. What was clear, when I saw my mother's face, was that we were home.

Eddie—as I prefer from here on to call my father—hadn't been informed of the time or place we were to land, only that our arrival was expected. From the R.A.F. canteen, where we were taken first for a cup of tea, my mother telephoned and told him that we were in Bournemouth and would be in London that evening by train. We had not seen him for two and a half years, and at the station where he was waiting, the appearance of his children clearly surprised him. I was a foot taller than when we'd left and nearly thirteen, and John, who had been still something of a baby in 1941, was now a clever boy of eight. I was happy to see Eddie, but terrifically shy and constrained, and also distressed that my mother would now have to share her affections with someone else.

There hadn't been an air raid on London for some months, but as we got off the train, the warning sirens sounded. It was the beginning of what was to be known as the Second Blitz.

Out in the blackout we got a taxi to Curzon Street. Eddie's fortunes had, as usual, fallen and risen by turn while we'd been away—in what enterprises I never knew—and he was now living in Mayfair, up in the world from the bungalow in New Milton. Just the foyer in Curzon Street was larger by far than our room in Forest Hills. And it was graced with a uniformed doorman. We went up in the elevator to a sparsely furnished flat with two bedrooms. It didn't look like a home, it looked like a hideout, and I didn't like it. I was to live there for the next ten years.

Though our own flat was anything but chic, the street was decidedly smart, inhabited largely by wealthy bache-

lors and rich divorcees and widows. It was only a block
from the Ritz, but as a child I didn't particularly want
to be living a block away from the Ritz. I wanted to be
living in a neighbourhood with some family feeling about
it, something, ideally, like Hampstead or Chelsea. I was
particularly embarrassed, when I began a few years later
to perform at the Old Vic, to have to say I lived in Mayfair,
since just about everyone else in the company lived a long
tube ride away.

A block away was the Ritz, and about a hundred
yards away, if that, was Shepherd Market: the prostitutes
standing in doorways and walking up and down with their
dogs, in all looking prettier and a good deal brassier than
most other women in wartime London. Diagonally across
Curzon Street from our building was the Washington Club
(now the Washington Hotel), an entertainment center of
sorts for American servicemen. They came to Curzon Street
to dance and drink at the Washington Club and to meet
the prostitutes in the street. They all drank a lot and whis-
tled at the girls and pinched just about everybody's behind.
I was a little scared of them, though they never did any
more than whistle at a girl as young as myself, and let
me pass by, untouched. The prostitutes didn't like to see
other women walking along the street, particularly after
dark, but I was recognised as a neighbourhood child with
no interest in the American trade, and was never insulted
or attacked. I still remember a terrifying evening fight in
Shepherd Market between two competing tarts. It was
unlike anything I would have been likely to see on the
streets of Hampstead or Chelsea.

Green Park was to one side of the Curzon Street building and Hyde Park to the other—all very lovely, except that there were anti-aircraft emplacements in both parks and the noise during the night raids was deafening. There was also a restaurant below us. It was too expensive for us to eat in, but you could hear the music at night, when the music was going instead of the guns, and you could smell the cigars when you got into the lift.

When we went to see my grandmother the next day, I felt the full relief of being home. She had lost her son Lewis during the great Blitz on London. Her husband had died after a long, painful illness, through which she had nursed him at home. Still she herself seemed as cheerful, and to me as wonderful, as ever. We went to see my Aunt Mary and my cousin Norma, who had also stayed in London. I was old enough now to realize how imposing a woman Mary was, and to notice how she intimidated my mother, who admired and respected her, and like almost everyone else, allowed Mary's to be the final word in any discussion. After Mary's career was curtailed by ill health in her thirties—and at the height of her success—she frequently told my mother of her terrible frustration and the desire she had to return to the theatre in any role, however small. "I am *not* a mother," she would announce in her stentorian voice. "I am *not* a housewife—I am an *actress.*" She was a brilliant woman and a rigid woman. Her views on sex, politics, religion, and literature were made known to all with great obstinacy and authority. Although she came to be deeply involved in the struggle for women's rights and in the P.E.N. Club, she said that nothing save acting meant anything to her. I remember listening with amazement to this confession from the strongest woman I had ever known. I had certainly never thought of her as a mother (I doubt if Norma had either), but I did see her as an extremely vigorous woman of the world. The friends who visited her flat—mostly emigré Jewish intellectuals—made conversation of a kind I had never heard before. I envied Norma, living so close to such people, and once I met them, wanted that part of her life for myself. Much as I valued my mother's good sense and quiet intelligence, I began to toy with the fantasy of being Mary's daughter, even as she, I now know, began to toy with the fantasy of mothering me and living out in my career her own cruelly frustrated ambition.

Back when we'd been living in Bristol, I'd had some lessons at the Cone School, a dancing school run by three sisters, Miss Lily, Miss Valerie, and Miss Gracie. My mother learned that they had opened a school in London, not far from us, where you studied dancing and theatre in the morning and took your regular school lessons in the afternoon. I was accepted, and, with that same excitement with which I began lessons at a dancing school anywhere in the world, resumed classes with the Cone sisters just weeks after our return. I had to buy tights and a leotard, tap shoes and ballet slippers. Most of the clothing ration for the whole family went into outfitting me. I had to have heavy hair nets. I had to have pink silk hair ribbons. At home I put everything on and looked in the mirror. I saw nothing less than Pavlova. It was worth everybody's ration stamps.

Of the Cone sisters, I remember Miss Gracie as the most inspiring teacher—among her pupils had been Anton Dolin and Alicia Markova. In my own class were John

Gilpin, the English classical dancer whose gift was apparent even then, and Natasha Parry, a slim girl, partly Russian, with beautiful long black hair, by far the prettiest girl in school, who became a fine actress and was to marry Peter Brook. Everybody seemed awfully beautiful or awfully talented, or what was more dispiriting, both.

We had a limbering class first, then an hour and a half of ballet, then tap, then musical comedy, then lunch, then the least serious part of the day, three hours of school. After school there would be extra ballet lessons, ballroom dancing, and acting. In acting class I gave improvisations based on the film *The Song of Bernadette.* I held the class of five spellbound with my visions, but was at my best in the last stages of terminal disease.

Aunt Mary didn't think the Cone School was good enough for me. She had seen a newspaper advertisement announcing a part-time scholarship for the Guildhall School of Music and Drama. Everybody else thought I hadn't a chance at only thirteen, but Mary told me to go in and lie about my age and see what happened. She thought at the least the lying would be good experience.

I went in, lied, and then did Saint Joan, and was offered the scholarship. I was stunned, not least of all because I was so happy at the Cone School. But if the place wasn't good enough for me, how could I argue, especially with Mary?

The Guildhall offered me two hours a week of private acting lessons with Dorothy Dayus. Aside from that, I would work on scenes to be performed at the end of each term. The scholarship was for a year. To fulfil my academic requirements I enrolled at a "crammers" school for students who had to fit academic studies around schedules like mine. The school, Carlisle and Gregson, called by all of us Rubble and Wreck, specialised in training boys for military academies. I was the only girl. Through her friend Ross Nichols, Mary had arranged for me to go there. Ross Nichols, a Rubble and Wreck teacher and a ballet critic, was, in fact, the person who got me to think about something other than *Swan Lake* and *Giselle,* and after taking his courses in Chaucer, Shakespeare, and English History, I finally got my school certificate—honours in English Language and History, and a failure in everything else.

In June 1944 the Germans introduced us to their new invention, the pilotless plane or V-1. The first night they came over, no one knew what they were, only that they were ominously different from what we had grown used to. The next morning we read in the papers that these were the first of the radar-guided missiles that Hitler had promised England, the "buzz-bomb." You heard the engine, a very distinctive sound—something like the engaged signal on the telephone—then it cut out, and you counted ten. If you were still alive, it had fallen elsewhere.

Rubble and Wreck had lost half of its roof—and it was winter. We had a small gas fire in the classroom, but it was scarcely enough. We broke at eleven for tea, and I would run straight to the local Lyons and gulp down a large piece of hot suet pudding with custard. I finished at Rubble and Wreck by 3 P.M. and by underground got myself down to Fleet Street, where the Guildhall then was. Taking my acting lessons in the old City of London made me feel closer to Shakespeare's England—not that it took the City of London to do that for me when I put my mind to it. All that term I worked in the late afternoons with Miss Dayus, playing Viola in the willow cabin scene from *Twelfth Night,* and then it was dark and I headed back out into the City, praying that the most ancient streets of London (and my family) would survive the evening's V-1 raid. More and more we were passing our nights in the corridor of our building, where we dragged our blankets and mattresses when the air-raid alarm went off outside. We were meant to be safe there from anything but a direct hit. I was too exhausted from all my lessons and classes not to sleep, corridor or no corridor, except when the bombs fell nearby or the anti-aircraft in the park began to sound.

Early on Saturday mornings I would join the queue outside the Old Vic to buy tickets for John, my mother, and me. I remember arriving as early as seven so that we would be sure to see Richardson's *Peer Gynt* and Olivier's *Richard III.* We would get seats in the Upper Circle, as it was then called—specifically, for the Upper Circle box, which was that much closer to the stage. True, you could see only one side of the stage from the box, but as we meant to see all the plays twice at the least, we would catch it from the box on the other side the next time round. The Sadler's Wells Ballet, with Margot Fonteyn and Robert Helpmann, had come back to London that season, so if I wasn't queuing up Saturday mornings at the Old Vic, I was outside Sadler's Wells.

I had been at the Guildhall a year, when, in 1945, the V-2's began. These were more terrifying even than the V-1's, as they were rockets that gave no warning of their arrival. They just flew soundlessly in and exploded.

Every time one was reported to have landed, I phoned home, certain there would be no reply. We were all so frightened again that Mary and my mother decided to send Norma and me to the country to a school in rural Oxfordshire, where Norma had gone as a child, but this seemed to me worse than staying in London. I should have to give up the Guildhall and I would just as *soon* be dead. Rather sulkily I trooped off with Norma to Euston Station, where for the first time I saw Londoners in panic. They were pushing and shouting to get their children on the only train going to the West that afternoon. We ourselves couldn't get on board a westbound train until the next day.

The school was in lovely country. Norma and I had a double room in a comfortable cottage next door, but I walked around with my return ticket in my pocket. And I quarrelled: with my mother on the phone, with the other children in the school, and with Norma, who finally threw a table tennis racquet at my head—after which I tore her shirt off her back.

In a month I was back in the Guildhall and back at Rubble and Wreck.

And then in May the war was over. Outside Buckingham Palace we stood and cheered with everybody else while the King and Queen, Princess Margaret and Princess Elizabeth came out onto the balcony. I would never have to leave London for Florida or Oxfordshire again. *I wouldn't budge.*

I was now fourteen, school-leaving age and legally free to go as a full-time student to a school of drama. I auditioned and was accepted at the Central School, the training ground for the Old Vic. I was still miserably shy, and the atmosphere at the Central School didn't help. Gwyneth Thurburn, the principal, was a very dour lady, and her assistant, called, ominously enough, Miss Sargent, ran the place like a panzer division. I was called "Bloom."

Shy—and yet audacious enough to write a letter at this time to John Burrell, director of the Old Vic, to ask if they were holding any open auditions. His secretary replied that they were and I was invited to attend. Burrell was kind to me, said after the audition that I was very talented, but obviously too young, and suggested that I take lessons with Sybil Thorndike's sister, Eileen. He even telephoned her himself. Two shadowy figures in the stalls during the auditions were Richardson and Olivier.

Miss Thorndike lived in Notting Hill Gate with her grown children. They all had that great Thorndike voice and those strong English faces. The Thorndikes were parson's daughters, and when I went for my lesson there once a week, after the day at Central was finished, we recited an awful lot of Bible in addition to our Greek drama. For myself, I became more passionate about Medea and Antigone than about Saul's lament over Jonathan.

One day John Burrell's assistant called and asked me to hurry down to the Old Vic, which was then at the New Theatre in St. Martin's Lane. When I arrived I was told to go on stage—and there was Laurence Olivier. He had his arm around a tiny, large-eyed girl called Jane Wenham, and I was told to stand on his other side, so that he could put his arm around me. I had been brought up by women and knew nothing about men, and when Olivier put his arm around me, I nearly swooned with excitement.

He was casting Ismene, Antigone's younger sister, in *Oedipus Rex.* Alas, I was nearly a head taller than Jane Wenham. "You've growed," said Olivier, and back to the school I went, "Bloom" once more, still Miss Thurburn's and Miss Sargent's instead of Laurence Olivier's.

At the end of the first term at the Central School we did some scenes from *The School for Scandal.* I did not excel. I played the maid and then Maria, and Maria in another scene and then the maid again. It was a system designed to give everybody a chance, but, with all the costume and makeup changes, it had me flying in every direction. When the scene was over and Miss Thurburn gave us our notes, she announced to me, in her intimidating fashion, "Bloom, your performance was acceptable, but your appearance deplorable." I went home cowed, as I usually did with my notes from Miss Thurburn. I was hardly a success at the Central School—certainly not until the next term, when I played Dina Dorf, a part I was suited for, in Ibsen's *A Pillar of Society.* Olive Harding, the theatrical agent, had come to the performance to see some older student she'd heard about, but afterward came to ask me if I would sign as a client with her. I accepted, and only a little later auditioned for the BBC's radio repertory company; I was told I was too young for the company, but was offered the role of Anne of Oxford Street, a prostitute in an upcoming dramatisation of DeQuincey's *Opium Eater.* I was only fifteen, but I wanted to do it, and went to ask permission of Miss Thurburn and Miss Sargent. Miss Thurburn was reading and didn't look up. Miss Sargent spoke for her, although I addressed all my questions to her superior, Miss Thurburn. Miss Sargent said I could choose either to go out into the professional world, for which I was not nearly ready, or remain at the school for a further two years of preparation that I desperately needed. Well, I didn't much care for the two of them, I didn't any longer like the school, I was ambitious, and we needed the money. Only months before, Eddie had decided to go off to South Africa to seek his fortune, without worrying much about ours, which at the time was negligible.

So I took the role of the prostitute. I was no longer the Central School's "Bloom," but a professional actress out on her own.

3

I Go to Work

I felt in full support of my family, and I probably was. I don't know what Eddie sent us, but it couldn't have been much. In my good weeks, I earned between twelve and fifteen pounds. The strange thing was that we lived quite well. I took on part of John's school fees—he was a day student at Westminster—and paid most of the rent, and I don't remember wanting for anything. Obviously there were things I couldn't have—that new dress, for instance, with which I would knock them cold. There was just such a dress in the window of Dickens and Jones: black silk, with a white collar and cuffs, and pearl buttons. Forty-five pounds. I looked at it every time I passed, until at last it was mercifully taken from the window.

One producer who employed me regularly at the BBC was R. D. Smith, Reggie to those who worked with him. Huge, bear-like, lots of curly hair, a round face and round glasses—an enormous, imposing figure, a man of exquisite taste and intelligence. He produced the programme called "This Is London," which opened with the announcer quoting Dr. Johnson: "When a man is tired of London, he is tired of life, for there is in London all that life can afford." We rehearsed in one of the BBC subterranean studios off Oxford Street. The programme was to go out overseas, wherever that may have been: Calais, New Zealand, the Isle of Wight? I never knew. Louis MacNeice was involved with the programme, as was C. Day Lewis, but I was so young I didn't realise who anyone was and took little notice of the noteworthy. One cherubic, drunken Welshman, whom I thought disgraceful, was Dylan Thomas. I hadn't any idea what the bits and pieces we did added up to—I only remember playing lots of little scenes in every accent I could manage: Cockney, Welsh, something I thought of as "country," something else I called "North." I went out with the cast after rehearsal to the BBC Club and drank lemonade shandy—and listened. I never once spoke, in any tongue or accent whatsoever.

Soon other broadcasts came my way: Nina in *The Seagull*, the third lady-in-waiting to Richard II—I even got a notice in *The Listener*, but if it was bad or good, I no longer remember.

In late 1946 Peter Brook had announced that he was searching for a fourteen-year-old girl to play Juliet at Stratford-upon-Avon. My Aunt Mary, in a brief return to the stage, had been directed by Brook when he was only nineteen, in a successful tour of *Pygmalion*, and I had met him once backstage after a performance of the play at Drury Lane. His eyes were astonishingly blue, attractive and deeply calculating. One felt one's capabilities—intellectual and sexual—summed up by them in a moment. When I came to work for him some years later, I imagined those eyes had the power to *frighten* you into being a better actress. I recognised in him, even though I was then only thirteen, the same powerful drive toward success that I felt growing in me. Mary was exultant at having been responsible for discovering him, for she had seen his production of Büchner's *Leonce and Lena* at the tiny Chanticlair Theatre, and immediately asked him to direct her *Pygmalion*. By the time I went to read for him as Juliet, his reputation had already been established at the age of twenty-one by a production of *King John* at the Birmingham Repertory, where he had formed a partnership as director–actor with Paul Scofield. I'm sure that he was amused by my unquestioning belief in myself at fifteen and I don't suppose that he had ever seriously considered anyone quite so young to play the part. Eventually he did choose an actress a few years older, but I must have made some impression, because he chose me four years later to play an excellent role in the West End, over the competition of many better-established young actresses.

Shortly afterward, Malcolm Morley, who was director of the Oxford Playhouse and who already had one ingenue in the company, announced two plays which needed two young actresses. Mary had worked with Morley in Strindberg's *The Father* and he asked her advice. She suggested me. Strangely, I don't remember any sense of great excitement this time, nor can I remember anything about the audition except that mixed with my ambition was my fear, equally strong, of leaving home to stay in a strange place for some nine weeks. I got the job, and was asked to play Private Jessie Killigrew in James Bridie's *It Depends What You Mean*, the second sister in *Pink String and Sealing*

Wax, and the bride in Labiche's farce *An Italian Straw Hat*. My mother took me down on the train and we stayed together for the first few days at a pub called The White Horse, fairly expensive for the salary I was to earn, but safer for me than "digs." The pub stank of stale beer, dreadful cooking, and gas fires; the rooms were icy and the fires were fed by penny-in-the-slot meters. But I was an actress and I was on my own; and though having my mother with me was a comfort, I felt foolish, now that I was a "professional," still to need her care—though once she had gone, the joy of being independent was subdued by daily bouts of lonely panic. My mother came up every fortnight to be sure that I was safe and eating and well. On the day of her first visit, I happened to be wandering across the road thinking of my great future when I was nearly knocked down by a bus. My mother was riding in it. This odd coincidence did not diminish her fears for the actress on her own.

As for my virtue, she had little to worry about. There was a young, attractive Welsh actor in the company, whom I had a crush on, but so did all the other women in the company and half the girls in Oxford. I hadn't begun to notice young men much. Boys of my own age I never noticed at all. I rather liked the idea—I rather nursed the idea—of bumping into some handsome undergraduate while on my walks by the college quadrangles. He would recognise me as the actress he had seen the night before and then sweep me away, or even just ask me to have tea. But nothing like that happened. I would have had no idea how to handle myself if it had. Everything I knew about the encounters of men and women I had read in nineteenth-century literature, by which I was corrupted early. Apart from my father, who had gone more or less out of my life when I was nine, I had no idea of what a man was or could be—or couldn't be. Byron and Heathcliff were the models who served my sexual imagination; after them, Mr. Rochester, M. Paul Emanuel, and Maxim de Winter.

All I can recall now about my first days of rehearsal was the familiar feeling of excitement, and then the sense of great pleasure—and the warm feeling of belonging— that I had as I walked back and forth to the theatre, a member of a respected repertory company. I doubt if I was well cast in the role of an assertive young private in the women's auxiliary army corps. I remember an almost paralysing self-consciousness about my movements, and also my surprise at the sound of my own voice in a large theatre on the first night. My costume, hired from the local army barracks, was too large and held together by safety pins which, one after the other, came painfully undone. The play was written in the form of a debate and had been confusing to learn—so confusing that on the first night we started the third act only to find we were repeating part of the first. I remember the feeling of panic— of my face boiling hot—and the fear that we would never get back to where we belonged. When somehow we did, I felt enormously proud: one performance and I had survived a "disaster" in the theatre.

I moved into a room in a private house near the river— a little colder, even cheaper, with breakfast thrown in. I made friends in the company and I discovered the city on my own. The colleges, the churches, the market places—every walk had its beauty, and I felt fortunate to be in lovely, ancient Oxford, rather than playing in the theatre of one of England's industrial towns.

So, at fifteen, a professional. As I was already playing adult parts, and for my age looked remarkably mature, I was spared the status—and the treatment—of the "child actress." But what I was, really, was a child who acted.

In the second play, an obscure comedy called *Pink String and Sealing Wax*, I performed as the daughter who wants above all to become an actress and is continually breaking into bits of Ophelia or snatches of old songs. This is commonly referred to as "playing yourself," and I knew it. I recalled the lines about Nina in *The Seagull:* "She had a certain talent for screaming and dying, and that was all." Could that be me? But mostly my self-confidence was unbounded. I assume I must have been reasonably awful. I had "exquisite" South Kensington elocution (I wouldn't lose that entirely until I had spent several years in America) and lots of enthusiasm. I was very young and pretty and had no idea what acting was about. My few years of training had given me some basic knowledge of how to conduct myself on a stage. I could "project" my voice, wait for a laugh, and sit in a period play without crossing my legs. I had no means, however, to analyse a character or to find the living, as opposed to the theatrical, reality in my role—I could only imagine in the most general way. I performed in the exhibitionistic sense of the word, and though I must have had some personal gift that managed to make itself apparent to an audience *despite* the conventions which I mimicked as an actress, I wasn't to be in touch with my own sense of things for years.

An Italian Straw Hat, the last play of the season, was a charming comedy with music and dancing. I had lovely clothes, or so I thought, and felt myself to be beautiful. Our makeup then was exaggerated to the point of the grotesque. When I had been taken backstage for the first time to see my Aunt Mary in her dressing room, I had stared speechlessly at her orange face, bright blue eyelids, crimson cheeks and at the red dots in the inner corner of each eye, placed there, I learned in time, to give the effect of brilliance. Though that style was connected to the techniques of self-projection—of voice and gesture— that had carried over from the nineteenth century, it was still the convention when I started my career. With the enormous shift, amounting almost to a revolution, toward natural or lifelike behaviour that took place in the English theatre in the fifties, makeup too became subdued and understated, so that today "straight" makeup is little different from what one would wear out in the evening.

On this particular first night, I did as most actresses and put "hot-black" on my eyes. We had no false eyelashes, and so used a stick of black wax that one melted in a spoon over a candle. After using mascara, drops of the stuff were balanced on the tips of the lashes, until you had built them up and out to doll-like proportions. At the first performance, the leading man looked at me strangely. Later, in the mirror, I discovered why—my lashes had smeared all over my face, and it must have appeared to him that I had entered down a chimney.

As no more parts for someone my age were on the
schedule, I went home to my first experience of the fear
that haunts all actors: I would never work again. I began,
at fifteen, waiting by the phone; I would not go out for
fear of missing a call. Sad, in a way, but also exactly what
I wanted. It was hard for me to have normal friendships
with unemployed boys and girls. I sought the excitement
of the theatre instead. My father's gambling instinct—the
form taken by *his* desire for excitement—has always been
an ingredient in my character, and for years I seemed to
win every time. Until my mid-twenties, it seemed I could
do almost nothing but win. Acting took the place of everything, including education; it *was* my education, the only
one I wanted.

John now began to find living with two high-strung
women more than a ten-year-old boy could take. Because
of the size of the flat there was little room for him to
play, no spare bed for a friend to sleep over, and no real
privacy for any of us. His cricket mania bored me and
to him my theatrical chatter had become maddening. He
asked if he could go to Westminster School as a boarder.
At first, I was sure that he would suffer too much, leaving
his home and his mother and sister. I didn't at all understand how much he needed independence. I accompanied
my mother on her visit to the headmaster, and we were
taken to see the Westminster School dormitories. Not even
my experience in "digs" had prepared me for the army
cots, the army blankets, and the institutional cream and
green walls. However, Westminster was the most liberal
of public schools, and one, in fact, with a strong theatrical
tradition, John Gielgud and Michael Redgrave being two

of its graduates. So John was enrolled, went off to school to live, and to my surprise, I missed him.

Finally the phone did ring. Olive Harding told me there was to be an audition at the Duchess Theatre, where Michael Benthall and Robert Helpmann were forming a new company. Their first play was Webster's *The White Devil* and the audition would be for walk-on and understudy.

For my audition, I did Juliet yet again, the "gallop apace" soliloquy. I hadn't yet tried it out in a theatre, and I was exhilarated when I found that the inhibitions I had felt, reading in a room for Peter Brook, vanished the moment I got up in a darkened theatre, aware of no one but myself. I knew they would take me—they did. I wore a dress whose colour I thought perfect, a deep bluish purple that did wonders for my pallor. By now I had begun to be obsessed with my looks, turning my head to catch a glimpse of myself in mirrors, shop windows, wherever I could find a reflection. I studied my "best" angles and got to know all of my faults, though not nearly so well as my "good points." This phase was a long time passing. My mother was questioned daily as to whether I looked pretty, or pale and interesting, or hideous.

The announcement of the season caused a stir in the West End—to open a little-known Jacobean play as a commercial venture was considered very daring. I was engaged to play one of Martita Hunt's ladies-in-waiting—the other was Heather Stannard. She was to understudy the leading lady, Margaret Rawlings; I was to understudy the romantic, hard-done-by younger heroine and also a sensuous Moorish waiting woman, a role in which I would have been quite funny had I ever been called on to perform it. Heather was given a line to speak in the prison scene, but she was much taller and remarkably beautiful.

Helpmann, though a great mime and dancer, had played only two parts before in the theatre, Oberon and Hamlet. He had enormous, prominent eyes set in a tiny face, his body was slight and precise in motion, and though his voice lacked resonance, it had a distinctive kind of power. It was his sheer theatrical flair that was magnetic, and because of it the transition from dancer to actor was easier for him than it had been for anyone else. Possibly he was neither a great actor nor a great dancer; beyond any doubt he was a great "homme du théâtre."

There was little discussion of the actual play at rehearsals. Benthall, like most directors of that period, was of the Tyrone Guthrie school: many theatrical effects, no investigation of the character or analysis of the play. Our production was beautifully decorated, and the set, of dark blue pillars veined in gold, did lend a dreadful mysteriousness to a play which reveals Webster as Eliot described him: "Much possessed by death, [he] saw the skull beneath the skin."

After a short tour the play opened in London to fine reviews. I was sure to be working for at least three months.

With Helpmann's guidance, my days fell into a new pattern. I began to go every morning for an hour and a half to the studio of the Russian ballet teacher Vera Volkova. Volkova was a tiny woman, then in her mid-forties, and nearly all the fine English dancers of that time studied with her, among them Helpmann and Margot Fonteyn. After the stolid worthiness of the Royal Academy approach, which was all I had been taught before, the openness of her interpretation of classical movement was new to me, and for the first time movement was connected to the realm of feeling. Of course I was tremendously excited to be working in the same class as Fonteyn and at barre always tried to sneak in behind somebody I could imitate. And there was Volkova, her every word wisdom to me. The boys were doing leaps, each straining to get higher than the other. "No, no, no," said Volkova. "When you leave the ground, yes you leave the ground, but you go *back* to the ground, because there is your root. Not trying to jump up in the air, but to keep to the ground and then to show you can leave it—there is your power."

She left England in the fifties to become principal teacher with the Royal Danish Ballet. In 1978, when I read in the newspaper that she was dead, I remembered the last time we had met, in 1950—I had opened in *Ring Round the Moon* in London and we had run into one another on a bus. "Ah, Claire!" she said. "I am so happy for you. I always knew you were an artiste—*not* a dancer, but an artiste."

During the run of *The White Devil*, I read that Laurence Olivier was looking for an Ophelia to play opposite him in his film of *Hamlet*. Jean Simmons had been announced, but she was no longer free—J. Arthur Rank, to whom she was under contract, said she couldn't do both *Hamlet* and *Black Narcissus*, the film she was about to begin. In desperation Olivier started to search for another actress and Helpmann told him about me. We were waiting in the cramped wings of the Duchess Theatre to go on stage when Helpmann called me over in his slightly teasing way, flirtatiousness half-disguised as heavily significant drama. In those days, there was a formal, clear-cut division between the leading actors and the junior actors in a company. One learned from them, one watched them, but you didn't get pally; you certainly didn't call Mr. Helpmann Bobby. I was stunned then when he took me aside and told me Olivier wanted to see me and there was a chance that he would test me for his Ophelia.

On a Friday I set off for Denham Studios, feeling as I had when we boarded the seaplane in the dark in Portugal: this is happening to someone else. Olive Harding took me in a car; it was as well that someone took me. Olivier, in his Old Vic performance as Richard III and his Heathcliff in the film of *Wuthering Heights*, embodied everything I thought of as "Byronic." The night before, to please this Byron, I had coloured my hair with henna which made it a light red, and I wore a white raincoat. I tried to look as ethereal as possible. I was taken to his dressing room. He didn't remember me, of course, from the Old Vic auditions. The room was huge by theatre standards, and I remember particularly a table full of manicure implements: the clippers, the scissors, so many surgical-looking instruments, and I as yet knew only the nail file. Olivier said he would like to test me and wanted to know how old I was. I said sixteen. He said he thought that was young, but he would try me. I was told to learn the nunnery scene over the weekend and to come back Monday. I somehow survived the weekend and that Monday a car was sent to drive me to the studio. Great care was taken to dress me properly and to give me a flattering makeup. I was taken down to the studio floor onto a large sound stage where only a few technicians were waiting. A small set suggesting a Renaissance room had been constructed. I was petrified to think that all this preparation was for me, but when we discussed the scene and Olivier told me how he wanted it played, I seemed to lose my fear; and when, finally, he read me the lines off camera and I played the scene as though to him, I knew that I was good, I knew this was my part and I felt it all was *meant to be.* Afterward Olivier told me he was enormously pleased and we would work on the role together during the coming week. He said everything to convince a novice that she had the role. In time one learns, but as I had told him, I was only sixteen. The next day I heard nothing. When Olive Harding rang the production office on Wednesday, they told her what a nice girl I was and how charming. That didn't sound good to me but I kept hoping. I didn't hear further, not even about my charm, all that week. The next Monday there was a picture of Jean Simmons in the *Evening Standard,* and an article announcing she would be Ophelia. He had managed to get her after all. I thought that nothing good would happen to me again.

At least I was still in *The White Devil* and had that daily ritual to rely on: coming in an hour before the performance, chatting with my friends in the company, making up; then the understudy rehearsals, matinee days, tea between shows; the heady feeling on a Sunday of being free. And of course, Friday, pay day.

I never played my understudy parts, perhaps just as well. But when Heather Stannard did—played Vittoria and got a laudatory notice from the great critic of the day, James Agate—that, coupled with my disappointment over Ophelia, was hard to take.

The White Devil came to an end, for a play of that kind a successful run of nearly six months. The next play was to be Leonid Andreyev's *He Who Gets Slapped*. There wasn't anything important enough for Heather in it, so she left. I was kept on to understudy the dancer, Consuela, played by Audrey Fildes, and to walk-on. I had hoped for more, but I was glad just to have been kept in the company. Helpmann was to play Prince and we were to be directed by Tyrone Guthrie. Guthrie was six foot six inches, his wife six foot four; if they weren't, they gave that impression to me. Very puritanical, very tight-mouthed, Guthrie had the searing kind of humour that is very funny if it isn't directed at you. The setting of the play is a circus and I walked on in various circus costumes: acrobat, dog trainer, Spanish dancer, and, in each, reacting as hard as I could to everything. But not hard enough, as it turned out. At the end of the second week, in front of the cast gathered together onstage for notes, Guthrie turned to me and asked if I thought I was leading the Puritan Maidens' chorus. The result was that from then on I could hardly move for fear that whatever I had done wrong, I might be doing again. I would go to rehearsals in agony—I could hardly find the courage to get on the bus for the theatre—and I cried at night when I got home. Of course I couldn't hand in my notice: we needed the money, I needed the experience, and to leave a production gave you a "bad name." Guthrie didn't fire me, as I feared he would—and then one day I had My Moment. It was during the scene when Helpmann was supposed to be dying. There was a long silence. I was holding a tambourine and I let it rattle just once, very faintly, and then fade away. I had thought it would sound wonderful and it did. Guthrie said, "Did you do that? Good, keep it in." He stopped picking on me and I felt I had finally done something on the stage, something of my own.

The opening performance was a disaster. There was a famous, rather elderly actor in the company, who played a leading part, and he had been away from the stage for several years. On the first night he forgot his lines. He kept saying, "Oh God, I can't remember," and beating his head with his fists. Helpmann tried to guide him with prompts: "But surely you remember, Count Mancini, when . . ." etc. Nothing helped. The notices were confused, most complaining that they couldn't follow the plot, which was scarcely surprising, as half of it had been left out. The management of the theatre panicked, contracted another play and immediately promised them the Duchess Theatre in two weeks' time.

Sadly enough, it was an extraordinary production. Doing a play under the constraining direction of someone so interested in theatrical effects as Guthrie could be stulti- fying, and yet the result was sometimes remarkable. In the short time we had left, the play was beautifully per- formed and the acting impeccable. I remember a striking ending to Act One, when Prince, the clown, alone in his dressing room before a performance, started to put white clowns' powder on his face. In despair he piled on more and more, until a cloud of powder filled the stage and the curtain came down on a white haze. The last night Helpmann made an eloquent speech to the audience, say- ing the play had been taken off without his consent and that the management had behaved contrary to theatrical principles, etc. All the actors were moved and the play closed.

I was well and truly "out of work." I sat by the telephone and moped and worried. I was sixteen. What if I
never worked again? Because of the Ophelia audition,
however, I was soon tested by Rank for various films.
But the parts generally ended up played by Jean Simmons.
Privately I hated the idea of films—I was sure that they
would corrupt me. But then Olive Harding phoned and
said that in spite of the tests I had thought so awful, J.
Arthur Rank had offered me a film contract. I didn't know
what to do. We were terribly hard up for money, but if
I accepted the contract I would never become a serious
actress—I'd be betraying my ideals. Generally it was childish thinking, but not altogether. I was right to fear films
for myself at that time, and, in fact, never really learned
to feel natural in them until I made *Look Back in Anger* in
my late twenties. Something always inhibited me, and the
ease that I was beginning to feel on the stage simply deserted me in front of a camera. I became self-conscious
about my looks, my bad angles, my figure, and though
this disappeared when I stopped going to see rushes, there
was still more to it than that. The entire discipline was
different. Hanging about for hours between one emotional
scene and the next, I hadn't the wherewithal to know
how to sustain my mood. And the emotion itself, which
came freely enough on the stage, had always to be forced.
To get tears to flow in a film, I remember sniffing at an
ammonia capsule, and when that didn't work, having
drops of glycerin carefully placed on my cheeks.

Nonetheless, I was offered a contract at twenty-five
pounds a week for the first year, rising to seventy-five
if the contract was renewed. A fortune to us, and so I
took it. I was cast to play Eric Portman's daughter in a

film called *The Blind Goddess*. The name of my character was Lady Mary Dearing—comical of course, since I knew as little of the aristocracy as they of me.

I took the bus to Islington at five-thirty every morning. I came to enjoy getting up to go to the studio before dawn and arriving before anyone but the makeup and hairdressing people were about. And I looked forward to my breakfast after the cold journey: bacon rolls and hot tea. For the film I wore hideous clothes, a cement hairstyle, and the orange makeup. The dialogue, very stiff-upper-lip, sounded unintentionally hilarious even then. I had no idea what I was doing. I had no idea how to hit a mark without looking at it, I knew nothing of film technique, and there had been no one as yet to teach me. And the notices for the film were as bad as we deserved. Of all the wooden actors, I especially was singled out. I never saw *The Blind Goddess*, but my mother did. She made no comment.

Not long afterward, I had a call from Michael Benthall, who was to co-direct, with Anthony Quayle, the next season at Stratford-upon-Avon: He told me he wanted me to audition for Perdita in *The Winter's Tale* and Lady Blanch in *King John*. I hadn't read either play, and immediately got out my red leather-bound Shakespeare that I'd bought on the instalment plan in Forest Hills. Lady Blanch, though she only had about twenty lines, was a role that appealed to me right off—what the critic Kenneth Tynan came to call "one of Claire Bloom's virgin sacrifice parts." The directors, in fact, wanted to see me for Ophelia, but hadn't told me because they thought it would make me too nervous. I went to the New Theatre, where I had gone with John and my mother every Saturday night for the Old Vic, and where I had seen nearly all the great plays I knew, and went onto that same stage. In spite of the initial secrecy, I had finally been told to prepare a scene from *Hamlet,* and Anthony Quayle acted it with me. It was high summer and I could feel my already elevated temperature rising from the heat. Afterward I was called down to the stalls and told that I had been auditioning for Ophelia and that the role was mine. I was to perform at Stratford, to act opposite Helpmann and Paul Scofield, in the part I had thought lost to me forever when it had gone to Jean Simmons in Olivier's film.

❧ 4

I Want, I Want, I Want

I am not at all sure that the best part in my life as an actress hasn't been the anticipation *before* a play, the pause to draw breath and rest, knowing that something important, something intriguing and difficult, was soon going to happen—but not too soon.

On the strength of the good news, we all went on holiday. I awoke every morning thinking: Stratford. Ophelia. Bloom.

On our return I went up to Stratford with Heather Stannard, who was to be the other younger leading actress, to look for digs. That Heather and I were already friends made everything less of an ordeal for me. We went to see a house called "Avoncliffe," owned by the theatre, set in lovely grounds two miles outside the town, near enough to bicycle or walk to rehearsal, far enough to leave everything behind if you wished. Heather had as little money as I had and we booked the two smallest rooms. Mine looked over a courtyard and honeysuckle grew outside my window: *mine*, to be shared with no one, to be the most peaceful room I had ever known.

We started rehearsals. I was rehearsing with not one, but two Hamlets, and with each alternately I thought myself in love. Scofield, whom I considered ancient, was possibly twenty-eight. He had a face already lined, evidence to me of secret vice. I suspect now that his viciousness didn't go much beyond a cream cake in front of the fire at the Anne Hathaway Tea Shoppe.

I came to the first rehearsal to play Ophelia, having read every footnote in the Variorum, and every book on *Hamlet* I could find. I was seventeen, Ophelia is surely little more. The part seemed easily within my grasp: to love desperately, to be rejected, to go mad, and to die. I think Benthall was amused by the amount of homework I had done and let me go about working the part out for myself. I remember that I couldn't find a way to begin the mad scene, couldn't connect it to anything real to me. I knew the shock of her father's death must have fallen like a wall between Ophelia and everything around her, but I had no idea how to demonstrate the magnitude of her displacement. In the third week of rehearsal I went into a shop and a woman, obviously mentally disturbed, came in, and pointing to something, said, "I want——I want—— I want . . ." but was unable to complete the sentence. "Where——where——where is the beauteous majesty of Denmark?"—and all at once I established for myself just how damaged was Ophelia's sense of time, place, and order.

We had consecutive first nights, the first featuring Scofield, the second Helpmann. I stood in the wings before my first entrance on the opening night, unknown and un-

tried, while in the audience were both my mother *and*
the critics. I had a deadly headache. I heard my cue, ran
down the steps in my flowing white and pale blue dress,
and heard the words that were to attend my entrances
for the next fifteen years. "Isn't she sweet!" It sibilated
through the house and I was enraged. I had expected they
would find me "dramatic" or "striking," not sweet. I
couldn't bear that I should appeal so much to the women
in the audience, and not in a quite different way to the
men.

The first night of *Hamlet* went well for us all. It must
have been a tremendous strain for Helpmann to follow
Scofield's success the next night, although it had been
his choice for them to perform in that order. The second
night of a play is difficult in any case—the second performance, to which critics also come, frequently feels flat
by comparison to the first. I remember no feeling of exhila-
ration, only a nervous stomach, and again a splitting headache and depression, all of which have become a standard
part of any opening for me.

The production was extremely handsome, set in the
mid-nineteenth century. In crinolines and a superb red
wig, Diana Wynyard, as Gertrude, resembled portraits of
the Empress Eugénie. While as Claudius, Anthony Quayle,
in military dress uniform and mutton chop whiskers,
looked like the Hapsburgs' most lascivious grand duke.

Both Scofield and Helpmann got excellent notices, and
I received my first good notice, from Alan Dent in the
old *News Chronicle*.

At the beginning of the summer, until all of the plays
were produced, we rehearsed during the day and played

With my mother and father

Age six, on holiday at the seaside

At about seven

At sixteen, my first film, *The Blind Goddess*, with Michael Denison, Nora Swinburne, and Eric Portman (*J. Arthur Rank*)

My aunt Mary Grew in the mid-twenties

As a nineteenth-century Ophelia at Stratford; Paul Scofield is the Hamlet (*Angus McBean*, *Harvard Theatre Collection*)

With Richard Burton in *The Lady's Not for Burning*, London, 1949
(*Angus McBean, Harvard Theatre Collection*)

In Peter Brook's production of *Ring Round the Moon*, 1950,
with Paul Scofield (*Houston Rogers*)

With Chaplin in *Limelight*, 1952

One of the backstage scenes from *Limelight* (© *Roy Export Co. Est.*)

With Alan Badel as Romeo at the Old Vic in 1952 (*Houston Rogers*)

As Lady Anne with Laurence Olivier in his film of *Richard III*, 1956

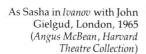

Lunching with Richard Burton
during the filming of *Look Back in
Anger*, 1959

Rod Steiger and I announce our
engagement, 1959

As Sasha in *Ivanov* with John
Gielgud, London, 1965
(*Angus McBean, Harvard
Theatre Collection*)

With Anthony Hopkins in the film of
A Doll's House, 1973

As Blanche du Bois in *A Streetcar
Named Desire*, London, 1974 (*John
Haynes*)

As Madame Ranyevskaya
in the Chichester Festival
production of *The Cherry
Orchard*, with Emrys
James as Lopakhin, 1981
(*Zoë Dominic*)

in the evenings. Each of us appeared in five of the season's six plays. My "play out" was *Troilus and Cressida,* in which Heather scored a great success. I couldn't bear my free evenings and would hang around in someone's dressing room or watch from the back of the theatre, waiting for after the performance, when we would gather for supper in the large dining room at Avoncliffe and discuss what had gone wrong with the play that night, who was sleeping with whom, who was likely to be asked back the next season, and why so and so was in the company at all.

That season I also played in *King John* as Lady Blanch, a perfect small part: a lost, pathetic character caught in the war between France and England. I walked on as a bridesmaid in *The Taming of the Shrew,* was an attendant on Portia, and played other walk-on roles in *The Merchant of Venice,* including a Venetian reveler with a funny nose who runs screaming around the stage—hardly what I thought of as my style. In the final play of the 1948 season, *Othello,* with Godfrey Tearle, I appeared for two minutes as a Cypriot woman. "Long live our noble general Othello!" I cried, and wore an off-the-shoulder blouse and curtain rings in my ears. With my hair long and frizzed, and covered in suntan body makeup, I felt my own ideal vision at last. It took me two and a half hours to make up.

In my other important role that season, Perdita in *The Winter's Tale,* I was a failure. I could discover little about her character and fell instead into reciting and posing. Everything was studied and "poetic," and I came to dread the evenings when that play was to be performed.

But I looked forward to everything else—even the long walks home along a deserted rural lane after the performance. Once I was accompanied for half an hour by a spectral figure in the hedge just beside me. This, I thought, is it: Young Girl Ravished on Country Road. When I had the courage to look back, I found I was being followed by a cow. We had picnics on Sunday nights when the weather was fine, and I was taken once for a row in a punt down the Avon. I enjoyed going into the country pubs that bore names evocative for me of Shakespeare's Warwickshire. I was in fact legally too young to be there, the only member of the company, except for the little boy who played Prince Arthur, still to possess a child's green ration book. That entitled me to one extra egg a week and a couple of bananas, but was otherwise a great embarrassment.

Our rations at Avoncliffe were augmented one week by a suicidal swan, who had strangled itself on the barbed wire near the house. It tasted gamy, but was a change from our diet of heavy puddings and pies. In every way I was having a good time, with no obligation other than to go to the theatre each night and do the thing I liked best in the world. What I couldn't bear was the thought of the season coming to an end.

Soon rumours of next season's programme started to filter down to the company, as they always do. There were parts I thought that I could play, but I waited in vain for the call to Anthony Quayle's dressing room. Michael Benthall, my real sponsor, was not sharing the directorship with Quayle the next season and it began to be obvious to me that I was not to be asked back. I comforted myself with the thought that Quayle wanted to choose his own actors, but I was heartbroken. I had so enjoyed being a professional and being an adult, and I was afraid that in the small flat in London Mama's Little Girl might prove a more impossible role even than Perdita. And I still worried that once *this* engagement was over, I'd never work again.

I arrived home—as miserable as I had expected—to learn that Rank had cancelled my contract. It was as I had wanted it, but the timing was wrong, and it only added to my insecurity. Not altogether an imaginary feeling either, as it wasn't clear where the next housekeeping cheque was coming from. My film contract had been an embarrassment to me, as I had to have "by kind permission of J. Arthur Rank" printed after my name in the programme at Stratford. At that time Rank had something called the "charm school," to which certain unfortunate young actresses were sent. No one had asked me to go there and nothing would have made me do so, but I was sure the programme note gave the press and public a wrong impression about all my ideals. In any case, that was over as well.

I sat by the phone and waited. For whom? For anyone and everyone: for my agent; for some employer who might by the merest chance have seen me, even just heard my name mentioned; I waited for my big break or for any little crumb.

It must have been hard for my mother to see me, at seventeen, doing nothing save mope around the house. She comforted me, told me that something *had* to happen eventually, and tried to get me interested in what was going on outside the small theatrical world in which I seemed determined to enclose myself.

Finally I received a call from Daphne Rye, the casting director for H. M. Tennent, the largest production company in London. They were to present *The Damask Cheek* by John Van Druten at the Lyric Theatre, Hammersmith. Daphne Rye had seen my Ophelia and wanted me to play the young girl. I knew enough not to turn down an offer from as powerful a company as Tennent's. I thought the part a come-down after my Stratford adventure—moreover I have never been good at playing delightful little things. I had never been a delightful thing myself, and it is hard to play someone with whom you have nothing in common. But to choose a role wasn't quite my privilege yet, and I considered myself lucky to have anything. I got off without anyone really noticing me, which was just as well.

Tennent's was about to produce *The Lady's Not for Burning,* a new play by Christopher Fry, who was beginning to attract some serious attention. The play had been presented originally at The Arts Theatre and now John Gielgud was going to direct and star in it in the West End. Pamela Brown would be leading lady and Oliver Messel was to design the sets and costumes—a prestigious production. I was told by Daphne Rye to go and audition for the part of Alizon Eliot, the young girl. I read the script and saw that she had only two scenes, but that they were beautifully placed and charmingly written. I was determined to get the role.

Hugh "Binkie" Beaumont, the managing director of Tennent's, was then the most powerful and distinguished figure in the London commercial theatre: elegant, charming, witty, extremely shrewd, one of the "gentlemen" of the theatre. I knew that I *had* to make a good impression on him. John Gielgud was of course one of my idols—I had seen his Hamlet, his Oberon, his Raskolnikov. How was *I* to impress *him?*

It was, for some long-forgotten reason, an early evening audition, giving me just time to get back to Hammersmith before the curtain rose. The lights were on in the front of the house and not only were Binkie Beaumont and John Gielgud standing on the stage, but Pamela Brown and Christopher Fry. I had not expected them *all* to be there. There was also a young man in attendance but as he was there to read as well, I scarcely noticed him at this, my first audition in the West End. We were introduced and then everyone—save the young man who was to read for the part of my suitor—went down into the stalls to listen to us. My partner seemed to be much more at home than I and even able to make a few feeble jokes. I could tell, however, by his shaking hands that he was as anxious as I was. We read our scene together and then I dashed off to my play, arriving about fifteen minutes before the curtain went up. At the end of the evening, Daphne Rye called: I had the part. I got out of the theatre, jumped on the bus, and rushed home to tell my mother and John. I remember that we all danced together in the living room.

The rehearsals began soon afterward. I met for the second time the young man whom I was to play opposite, Richard Burton, a Welsh actor, and I realised at once how extraordinary he was. I had been so intimidated by the notables gathered to hear us read together that I had scarcely given him a glance the first time we met. However, even in my state of shock, I had recorded the green eyes.

To Richard, everything seemed to come easily. His eyes on stage were mesmeric, giving him, even in repose, absolute command over an audience. In time I became envious of that control; he seemed to achieve it by doing *nothing.* At twenty-four he was recognisably a "star," a fact that, strangely enough, no one seemed to question, least of all Richard. At rehearsal Gielgud never tired of pointing out the difference between our ways of working, mine studied, his natural and relaxed. I knew there was a great deal of artifice in this casual manner of his; nonetheless there was nothing that he did that I could *see.* He just *was,* and there didn't seem any way that I could emulate that. Gielgud was anxious about this play and desperately wanted it to be a success. He became more and more short-tempered with us all, until one poor actor who contracted a severe case of jaundice—seemingly as a consequence of the pressure—had to give up his role, and to my knowledge was never heard of again. I came in for a nice share of this disapproval. "Do watch Richard and *try* to be natural!" So I became tighter and tighter until *I* managed to get the flu and was put to bed. I was sure that Gielgud would take this opportunity, now so conveniently given to him, to fire me. However, when I came back to work, I met him outside the stage door, where he raised his hat to me and said, "I hope you're feeling better. I am so glad you are back. We missed you." "Well," I thought, "I suppose I am here to stay."

For *The Lady's Not for Burning,* set in the Cotswold Hills in the middle of the fifteenth century, Oliver Messel had designed a magnificent Gothic room, with one huge win-

dow at the centre. There through the first act John Gielgud
stood as Thomas Mendip, actor, while as J. Gielgud, director, he watched us all, those blue eyes missing nothing.
My mother claims that at the first performance in Brighton,
she fell into such a state of terror at the way his gaze
never moved off me that she had no idea at the end what
my two scenes had been about.

I shared a dressing room with Nora Nicholson, a distinguished actress in her early sixties, devoutly religious,
an old friend of Gielgud's and most patient and gentle
with me. When Mac, Gielgud's gentleman's gentleman,
would come up to the room we shared together and tell
me that Mr. G. wanted to see me in his dressing room, I
would fall into a panic. Nora would then calm me, and
shoo me off downstairs, where I would be told that there
had been complaints again from the audience that I was
not being heard. It seemed Gielgud could never remember
my name, for he would ask Nora from time to time how
"the little girl upstairs" was getting on. That came to be
Nora's pet name for me, and we used it when she played
my nurse in *A Doll's House* twenty years later.

We were on tour with *The Lady* for eleven weeks, and
worked on the play the entire time, with Fry rewriting,
generally from suggestions given by Gielgud. We played
the dismal places, but some of interest to me as well: Oxford, Newcastle, from where I travelled to Durham Cathe-
dral, and Brighton, which I always enjoyed. Burton and
I developed a friendship and would read poetry endlessly
to each other in our digs. I improved somewhat as Alizon,
for I was called down to the star dressing room with less
frequency. The audiences seemed to enjoy the play, and

we arrived back in London in a success.

My social life in London was at this time nonexistent. Neither grown up nor a child, yet earning my own living, I fitted into no known category that young men could manage—or that I could. I frightened admirers away—and I don't remember too many of them—by my intensity. If a man wasn't an "artist" I had no time for him, even as a friend. I gave the impression—not a false one either—that my ideals were so high no one could hope to satisfy them. I lived only to get to the theatre in the evenings and I don't remember being in any hurry to get home after the show. Richard and two other younger actors in the company let me hang around with them in the pubs after the curtain had gone down, treating me in public like a mildly idiotic younger sister. I was just eighteen. I was allowed a lemonade while they drank their beers and then they saw me safely onto the bus home. That was the extent of my evening's excitement, and it completely satisfied me. It was the perfect uncomplicated life: my fifteen pounds a week, my mother's approval, and no love affairs. It is the very opposite, of course, of what outsiders think, but if you start in the theatre as an adolescent, you live those early years very much like a girl in a convent. There is only the work, and about everything else one remains hopelessly ignorant for far longer than most young women who seemingly lead less exciting lives. I could tell, even so, that I was attractive to people. I knew that though I had no formal education I was bright and quick to pick up new ideas, and I was determined that nothing should stand in the way of my success. I felt, as young people do, that I had infinite time in which to accomplish anything I wanted, although I did suspect that one day I would reach the age of thirty-seven, a figure which for some reason seemed to hold enormous dread. But even thirty-seven seemed too remote to worry about.

Although these were among the most pleasant years of my life, for my mother they were hard times. In South Africa Eddie had met a woman whom he wished to marry and he wrote to my mother saying that if she would not grant him a divorce, the small amount of money he sent us every month would be discontinued. On the other hand, if she did as he asked, he would be in a position to help us more than before. His intended wife, he said, was a wealthy woman. My mother felt she had no choice but to grant him a divorce. This involved further humiliation, as Bertha, the next lucky Mrs. Bloom, came from an orthodox Jewish family who insisted the divorce be granted both in a civil court and in a religious court with a rabbi officiating. After agreeing to these proceedings so deeply repugnant to her rationalist convictions and her own restrained bearing, my mother was more depressed than I had ever known anyone to be in my life. Eddie's new relations, not so naive as he must have thought them, prevented Bertha's share of the family money, which was considerable, from passing into his hands.

During the run of *The Lady* in London, rumours began to go around the theatre that Peter Brook was to direct a new play, *L'Invitation au Château* by Jean Anouilh, that Paul Scofield was to play the lead, and that there was a splendid part in it for a young actress.

My hopes rising and falling by turn, I waited to learn more. Finally I was told by Daphne Rye that Brook wanted to hear me; I was given a script and told to study two scenes. When I read the play I knew that unless Brook got a more established young actress, I would have a strong chance. A penniless young dancer—waif-like and frail, as only an Anouilh heroine can be—is brought to a country house and involved in a plot contrived by a wicked twin (with whom she falls helplessly in love) to seduce his innocent brother. Scofield was to play the twins, Margaret Rutherford to play a kind of fairy godmother, and Audrey Fildes a spoiled young millionairess. Oliver Messel again was to design the sets and costumes.

I learned my scenes and went to the audition. Scofield said how lovely to see me again, and everyone was very kind, but by now I was beginning to realise just how much theatrical charm meant. Brook scarcely said a word, and when I left I had no idea how the audition had gone.

I heard nothing about the play—now retitled by the adapter, Christopher Fry, *Ring Round the Moon*—for over a month, other than that Jean Simmons had the role, and then Siobhan McKenna—the latter the usual case of misreporting, as she was to star in a different Anouilh play altogether. Even so, I never lost the sense of anticipation when I awoke each morning, that on that day I was to hear my great news. By the fifth week, when even *my* optimism was beginning to fade, there was a phone call for me on the public telephone in the hallway during the last interval: Daphne Rye to tell me that Peter Brook had made up his mind. I started to cry, and had time just to call my mother before I ran downstairs to go onstage for the last act.

Esmé Percy, who appeared only in the last scene to

play a flamboyant drunk, had some years earlier lost an eye while playing with his dog, and so wore a glass one in its place. As he approached me that momentous evening, the eye fell out directly at my feet. "Pick it up," he whispered to me. I stood there paralysed, quite sure that if I looked at him I would see through to the back of his head. Another actor, who, unlike me, had been trained as a doctor, miraculously happened to be onstage as well, and handed it back to him. Esmé stuck it back in his skull and went on with his scene unfazed by the episode. Afterward he was asked by John Gielgud to please wear an eye patch so as to prevent it from happening again. He did, though on certain playful evenings would decorate this with the *drawing* of an eye. When his glass eye did come loose on another occasion, it remained suspended this time on his cheek, held precariously by the decorated eye patch. It was like being on the stage with a Picasso.

We were to start rehearsals for the new play in a month's time. That meant that at the end of eight weeks I would have to leave *The Lady's Not for Burning,* and that I wouldn't be able to appear in the production if it went to New York.

An announcement was published in the papers for the new play, and my billing, under the title, was small and badly placed. When I went for my nightly visit to the boys' dressing room, I was asked if this had been upsetting. "Oh no, let *them* discover me," I said. No one in that room spoke to me for three days after—"to teach you humility," I was told by humble Richard Burton.

I left the play feeling lost and bereft. The end of a run is unpleasant under any circumstances, but it seemed worse to leave knowing that everything would be going on as usual the next night, with someone else wearing my clothes and saying my lines. I wanted to be able to do everything at once, the new play *and* the old. Frankly, I wanted *The Lady* to finish then and there, and not to have to part with anything.

I scarcely remember any of what Peter Brook said to me at rehearsal, certainly nothing extraordinary—strange, because he is now the great director of the English theatre. Yet the result of our work was magical. The curtain rose on a conservatory of Oliver Messel's exotic flowers. The romantic story worked charmingly from the first moment and it was clear immediately that we were a success. We played only two weeks in Brighton and then were to go into the Globe Theatre; *The Lady* was indeed on its way to New York and we were to take its place there.

Ring Round the Moon was a triumph. When Soho still possessed some charm, it was a pleasure to go to your evening's work by way of Berwick Street and Old Compton Street, passing the fruit and vegetable stalls and the Italian grocery shops. Most of the company used to stop at a coffee shop called Taylor's for a sandwich before the show, and I would look around to see if Paul Scofield was there. He was remotely friendly, as ever. I couldn't believe he was as delighted to see me as he said, but as long as I could sit next to him I didn't care. I was happy both in and out of the play.

I began to get some attention from the press. Photographs of me appeared in *Vogue* and *Harper's Bazaar*. Heather Stannard, who had a fine part opposite Olivier in another Christopher Fry play, *Venus Observed*, was being noticed as well, and so, as the two rising young actresses of the season, we were pictured side by side in top fashion magazines. We played through the summer, but I don't remember envying anyone his holidays. I had my nineteenth birthday on a matinee day, and was delighted to have two shows that day instead of one. I attracted my first admirer, titled, rich, much older than I. I dreaded going out with him, though he was intelligent and cultivated. When we went to the country to visit his friends, the back of his car was full of books. It seemed we were to improve ourselves and not waste time. This was not my idea of romance. I was taken to meet his mother. She must have approved of me, for on the way back he asked how I would feel about giving up my career. I replied that I should sooner die. Shortly after, I read that he had become engaged to another young lady.

While at the theatre, I received a phone call from Arthur Laurents, the American playwright. Charlie Chaplin was about to make a new film and Laurents had suggested me for the leading lady. I was to send Chaplin some photographs of myself—Laurents gave me an address in Hollywood which I copied down. If he had told me Shakespeare was interested in me, I would have found it equally believable.

I did nothing. I forgot the whole thing, so overwhelmed by the idea that I put it out of my mind. Everything was so good I wanted nothing to change. But a few weeks later I received a wire: "Where are the photographs? Charles Chaplin." No one could believe how careless I had been and I couldn't explain it, not even to myself. I could only say that I couldn't seriously believe that Chaplin had heard about me and so had discounted the whole matter. But that was only part of the truth.

I collected some pictures and sent them to Hollywood. I don't suppose I ever expected an answer. I didn't know that the part had been written for an English actress, that Chaplin wanted someone small, dark, and very young, and that, strangest of all, I bore, at least at that period of my life, an extraordinary resemblance to his wife, Oona.

Two weeks later I received a phone call backstage. It was from Harry Crocker, Chaplin's business manager. Chaplin had seen the photographs and wanted to test me for the part. Could I fly to Hollywood? I was terrified now that the management of *Ring Round the Moon* wouldn't release me—it was their right not to. It meant rehearsing an understudy to take over my part for at least two weeks. I couldn't reach anyone that evening and got no sleep, for now I wanted to be in that film just as strongly as two weeks before I'd wanted it not to happen. In the morning I called Olive Harding, and she, as excited as I, called Binkie Beaumont to get the necessary permission. He said he could release me for one week only. I knew that wouldn't be enough to travel all that way, and in despair wired the news to Hollywood.

Harry Crocker then called and said that Chaplin would come to New York by train—at that time he would not fly—and meet me. It would be possible to make a test within a week.

As I was nineteen it was arranged that my mother as chaperone would accompany me. Apart from any other consideration, Chaplin didn't want any gossip in the press about him and still another young actress. We were to fly to New York and stay one week. There Chaplin was to meet us, I was to rehearse with him for five days, and then we were to make a test together.

Harry Crocker told me that if I got the part, I would play opposite Chaplin himself, that the girl was supposed to be a dancer, and that the title of the film was to be *Limelight.*

Articles about me immediately began appearing in the press, all very flattering, but I feared—not altogether foolishly—that if after all that I wasn't Chaplin's choice, the newspapers would have their fun with me. Naturally I had to explain to Margaret Rutherford, Paul Scofield, and the rest of the cast why I would be leaving the play for a week. That Chaplin should have summoned a relatively unknown young girl all the way from England to America seemed as astonishing to them as it had first seemed to me.

When the day to leave came I was less frightened even of the plane journey than of the arrival in New York. I still hadn't read the script; Chaplin, understandably suspicious of everyone at that point, wouldn't allow me to have it ahead of time. His political position in the United States was already difficult, and his latest film, *Monsieur Verdoux,* had been treated cruelly by the press. Just how difficult life was for him there I as yet had no idea.

Over Newfoundland I began to hope that Chaplin's train would be delayed and he would arrive in New York a day late. Anything to put off the meeting. But after we landed and came through customs and into the entrance hall, there, quite alone, stood a slight white-haired man, fidgeting nervously. "Thank heaven, you're safe! I have been torturing myself in case anything should happen to your plane, when I was the cause of your journey." It was Chaplin. His face was tanned from the California sun and his blue eyes were remarkably clear. Concerned, kind, charming—no one could have less resembled the figure I had been fearing.

We were to stay at the Sherry Netherland Hotel, where Chaplin was. As soon as we were in the car for Manhattan, he began to talk with excitement about the film. He said the love story—so he described it—took place in the London of his childhood. The opening scenes were in the Kennington slums where he was born. The agents' offices where he had endlessly waited for work, the dressing rooms in the dreary provincial theatres, the digs, the landladies—all his melancholy theatrical memories were to be the film's backdrop. He reminisced about the Empire Theatre, the smart music hall of its day, frequented by the smartest courtesans; he talked of his early triumph as a boy actor in a stage adaptation of *Sherlock Holmes*, and then we arrived at the Sherry Netherland, I looking far from smart and achingly conscious of it. When we went to his rooms for lunch, he continued with his memories of London and seemed desperate to hear that nothing he had known had changed. In the last few years he had been deeply homesick, he said, but he didn't dare to leave America for fear that the U.S. government wouldn't allow him to reenter the country. His family, home, studios, money—everything was in America.

I was fascinated, not solely by him, but now by my mother's uncharacteristic animation. She was talking too about her youth, of the London Chaplin remembered as a young man and that she remembered faintly as a child. We had travelled over fourteen hours and she didn't in the least seem tired.

Later that afternoon my mother and I went up to our room to rest and change. We were joined at dinner by Jerry Epstein, who was to be assistant director of *Limelight* and who had accompanied Chaplin to New York to help him with the test. Chaplin said he had expected us to order the hugest steaks—it had been years, after all, since we'd seen steak at home—and he was amused when we had Dover sole. I realise now how brave it was of him to be out in a public place at that time in America. People dining at the other tables couldn't stop looking his way and expressing their opinions of him, ranging from adulation to loathing. Chaplin took no notice and told us about his wife, Oona. He spoke of her loyalty and devotion to him throughout the political ordeal. She was expecting their fourth child, otherwise she would have travelled with him to New York. He said that in Oona he had found a woman with whom he was completely happy.

Arrangements were made for me to go to his suite and rehearse in the morning. He relented enough to tell me that the next day I would have the full script to read and not just the two scenes we were to work on. I could not take the script to my own room, however, but must return it to Jerry Epstein every night.

Chaplin was the most exacting director, not because he expected you to produce wonders on your own but because he expected you to follow unquestioningly his every instruction. I was surprised at how old-fashioned much of what he prescribed seemed—rather theatrical effects that I didn't associate with the modern cinema.

We rehearsed from ten in the morning until six at night; I was to know the scenes the day after I was given them, and I did. I had the feeling that Chaplin was using this time to work through things for himself as well as for me. This film was, in its way, new for him too: serious, romantic, "straight." I listened to hear anything that would indicate if I was seriously in the running, but Chaplin was careful never to commit himself. Jerry Epstein confided to me that a few months back Chaplin had been in such despair of finding the right girl that he had placed an advertisement in the newspapers to the effect that he was searching for a young actress under five foot five who had some experience of acting and could give the impression of being a dancer. It seemed to me that if he had gone that far and still not found anyone, I stood a good chance.

My chances. I went over them with my mother a thousand times, my moods wildly fluctuating within the minute, between certainty and hopelessness.

In the evenings Chaplin would take us and Jerry Epstein to dinner at the most elegant restaurants. At the Pavillon and the "21" Club he spoke endlessly of his early poverty; the atmosphere he was creating for *Limelight* brought him back night after night to the melancholy of those years at home with his mother and brother. He spoke either of the early poverty or of his troubles with the U.S. government, troubles I wasn't quite able to grasp until I had spent a while in Hollywood.

We went to a theatrical costumier to outfit me for

the test. Chaplin had already decided upon every last detail of every garment I was to wear. He remembered the way his mother had worn such a dress and the way his first girl friend had worn such a shawl, and I quickly realised, even then, that some composite young woman, lost to him in the past, was what he wanted me to bring to life. He and Jerry were embarrassed when they realised one night at dinner that no one had seen my legs. If I was to be cast as a dancer, they certainly had to see my legs, but you can't ask a girl with her mother to raise her skirt in the "21" Club, or couldn't in 1950. So Chaplin suggested I try on a tutu and tights the next day, although we were to film no dance sequence for the test. I knew what it was about, they knew that I knew, but propriety prevailed.

We were to leave for London on Sunday afternoon and so we did the test on Saturday. We filmed at a little-used television studio and shot on a small sound stage, Jerry directing Chaplin and me. I was trying out for the role, Jerry hoped he would please Chaplin as assistant director, and Chaplin was watching the script he had worked on for three years finally come before the camera, so everyone was tense. I was close to panic: I hadn't retained much of value from *The Blind Goddess*, and had learned nothing more about film technique since. I was close to panic, however, only until I saw that Chaplin intended to give me every inflection and every gesture exactly as he had during rehearsal. This didn't accord with my high creative aspirations, but in the circumstances it was just fine. I couldn't have been happier—nor did I have any choice. Gradually, imitating Chaplin, I gained my confidence, and by the time we came to the actual filming I was enjoying myself rather like some little monkey in the zoo being put through the paces by a clever, playful drillmaster. I felt when it was all over that my big sentimental scene—the scene where the girl finds out that she will walk again—could have wrung the coldest heart. But I could tell nothing about Chaplin's heart at the end of the day, nothing at all about him other than that he was exhausted. Privately Jerry told me that Chaplin was pleased and furthermore had become very fond of me; but in the week we had worked together I had come to realize that Chaplin was a man who could alter an opinion without explanation, and that however much he liked me personally, and I thought he did, sentimental considerations would never intrude upon his work.

We all went for a farewell dinner, and when a friend of his stopped at our table, Chaplin said that he wanted him to meet a "marvellous young actress." That lifted my spirits more than a little. I could use it by then, for inevitably, now that my trial was over, I had begun to feel hollow and depressed. Having had a taste of splendour and glamour and fame, I didn't want to give it up. I had even begun to feel that I was an essential part of *Limelight*; no more than I could accept the idea of death could I believe that this might be the last evening I would ever spend in Chaplin's world. But Chaplin was taking the footage we had shot back to California, where he would watch it with Oona and his associates, and it would be at least ten days before there was anything to hear.

We landed in London on Monday morning and I returned to *Ring Round the Moon* that night. I was so young and strong and excited that I didn't feel at all tired after the strain of the last week and the long journey home. All I wanted was for the day to pass so that I could get to the theatre and tell my friends in the company all that had happened to me in New York. It never occurred to me that they might be less than thrilled to hear that while they had been playing for a week with my understudy, I had been hobnobbing with Charlie Chaplin at "21."

The return was a letdown, though not entirely as I had anticipated. Everything in my dressing room had been moved to make room for my understudy, and when I heard that she had given a lovely performance, I realised that I hadn't been missed very much. Then when I started to talk about New York, somebody changed the subject. Only Margaret Rutherford took me aside and asked to hear every detail.

The end of that week came, then the end of the next, and I heard nothing. And our flat did indeed look poor and miserable to me after the suite at the Sherry Netherland. Then John came home from school on the weekend and we argued constantly. Then I began going to the cinema in the afternoon to get through the afternoons. There was a rumour that *Ring Round the Moon* would play on Broadway and I told myself that therein lay my consolation. I wanted now to return to New York even if I didn't get the role in *Limelight.* I was convinced that the only exciting future I could ever have would be there.

Three weeks passed; in the fourth week, which I was sure would be *the* week, a wire came from Harry Crocker, Chaplin's business manager, saying that I would hear further within the next fortnight. One moment this seemed to me proof that I would be cast in the film, the next that I was ruined. The two weeks passed, then three, then four. Then the *Daily Express* printed the article I had been waiting for, saying that Chaplin had spent great sums to fly me to the States, that he was disappointed in my test, and that dozens of terrific young actresses were currently making their way through his studios.

After two months I began to forget my disgrace, sometimes for as long as an hour at a time. I only wished I had been told something, not left completely ignorant of why I had failed. *Ring Round the Moon* was continuing to run in the West End, although we had already been playing nearly eighteen months. Marie Lohr took over from Margaret Rutherford, but otherwise the company was still together. H. M. Tennent were convinced enough of my talent to sign me to a contract to appear under their management in my next three plays, and my future, at least for a few years, seemed as secure as an actress's can be. If it hadn't been for the misery over *Limelight,* I would have been so happy.

And then, four months after the test, Harry Crocker called Olive Harding from California and Olive Harding phoned backstage for me. My reaction was the same as it had been when I learned I had the role in *Ring Round the Moon:* trembling, terror, tears. I still remember telling Olive to please thank everyone for me but that I preferred to stay where I was. Olive said that perhaps I would feel differently in the morning. She told me the terms of my contract—enormous sums of money, certainly for us. I would be receiving fifteen thousand dollars for three months' work, plus our travel expenses and a generous weekly allowance for my mother and myself in California.

Strangely, my mother and I sat up all that night worrying, particularly about John. Neither of us thought that I was someone who could manage alone in Hollywood, but if mother was to come with me it would mean leaving John in his boarding school for the three months I was working. We couldn't stop thinking how long that could seem to a boy of fifteen.

The next morning I was still worrying—now about asking Binkie Beaumont's permission to leave the play, this time for good. But this he kindly and willingly gave, and it was even agreed that upon my return I would appear as the Queen opposite Paul Scofield in *Richard II.* I think the pleasure began when we discovered that there was enough money in the bank for me to buy one beautiful dress to take with me to Hollywood. I went to Victor Stiebel, I bought the beautiful dress, and there in the fitting room had the first full realisation of what had happened.

This time we were to travel by sea to New York and then by train to California. Olive Harding accompanied us to Southampton. On the train down someone who had seen my picture in the paper asked me for my autograph. That had never happened before and I, with my ideals, was outraged.

❧ 5

"O Fortune, Fortune, All Men Call Thee Fickle"

I had been fearing, altogether mistakenly, that because I was to be in a new Chaplin film the press was going to turn out in droves to meet us. What I still didn't understand was how unpopular Chaplin had become in America for his "Communist" activities. He was later to remark to me that the only Communist activity he'd ever engaged in was following each day, in the *New York Times,* the fluctuations of the stock market, though not in the hope of seeing a crash.

Without the press to detain us, we left New York for California on the Twentieth Century Limited. In Albuquerque, during a half hour stopover, my mother and I got so carried away by the beaded moccasins and the turquoise bracelets that we barely managed to make it back onto the train, even with the help of an irate porter. That was about the only half hour of the journey when I wasn't thinking about *Limelight.* On the day we were to arrive, I awakened long before dawn and sat for hours at the edge of my bunk, dressed and ready, waiting to see the California sun.

At Los Angeles we were driven by an aide of Chaplin's from the train to the Beverly Hills Hotel; there I was able to rest during the day before readying myself for dinner with the Chaplins at their house that evening. My mother, who had also been invited, characteristically declined to accompany me. She was there as a chaperone, she said, and did not intend to start hovering around as a mother. At eight I went down to the lobby, where Chaplin was waiting. "You will have to diet," were virtually his first words. I had thought my weight okay, but of course I was to play a starving girl. "We will both have to diet," he added, somewhat softening the blow. His small, tanned hands never stopped moving—not even while he was driving—as he described how he had planned my days for me. I was to go with his wife Oona each morning at nine to her exercise class, then to his house, where we would rehearse our scenes together from eleven until four, then to a ballet class for the next hour. There would be no lunch. This he strongly underlined. "For *either* of us." That was to be my regime for the next five weeks until we began the shooting. It sounded fine to me. Only what classes was I to attend between five in the afternoon and nine in the morning? I wanted even more to do. Because he had chosen me, my confidence was now boundless. All I wanted to show him was how right he'd been.

All the time he was prescribing how I was now to live, Chaplin was driving in his slightly erratic way up Summit Drive, a road then quite unspoiled, that could have been anywhere on the Mediterranean coast. We passed only one house, "Pickfair," built by Mary Pickford and Douglas Fairbanks, Sr., who together with Chaplin had founded United Artists, the basis of all their fortunes.

We turned into a long drive which led, on this California stretch of Mediterranean coast, to a white English country house.

Within, it was traditional, comfortable, and welcoming, the decoration of a style I came to associate with Chaplin, for he recreated it again in his house in Switzerland: dark green striped Regency wallpaper, a dark wood balustrade, vitrines displaying Staffordshire and Walton china, English furniture of the best Regency period. Oona Chaplin appeared to greet me—appeared dramatically enough to satisfy even my expectations—at the top of the stairs, wearing a green velvet gown that offset her dark Irish colouring. Chaplin had told me that they had first met when she came to audition for a role in a film he was planning but had never made. Only months later, at the age of eighteen, she had married him, abandoning all thoughts of an acting career to look after the private side of his life and to bear the first of their eight children. I thought, *Wife of a genius?* Another possibility for myself. The other guests were Jerry Epstein, Chaplin's assistant director, and Chaplin's son by a former marriage, Sydney. *Wife of a genius's son?* No, genius's leading lady sounded best of all.

We went in to dinner, and I was confronted with that perennial invitation to youthful disaster, the finger bowl. Though I didn't make the mistake of lifting it to my mouth, I had no idea what it might be there for and waited until I saw Oona put it to one side. Thus began a long course of watching Oona.

It was astonishing to discover how alike we two were. I could understand on that very first night Oona and I met why Chaplin had invited me to come for a test on the basis of the photographs I'd sent to America. The physical resemblance was at this time strong enough to confuse people into congratulating me on my husband and Oona on her performance. Oona and I both tended toward shyness and could comfortably sit through a social evening letting others do the talking—could probably only be comfortable knowing that it would not be we who would be called upon to entertain. In the presence of Chaplin's enormous personal force Oona could seem withdrawn and even self-effacing—yet she was to show extraordinary courage during the first years of their expulsion from the United States, and again during the last difficult years alone with her ailing husband in Switzerland. "When I was young," she told me during his illness, "he took care of me. Now I take care of him." Our reticence drew us together even in California, but our lasting friendship began when I left for England and we could correspond. Letters enabled two such shy young women to reveal how fond of one another they'd become, and to make it much easier the next time they met to show this fondness directly.

At dinner Chaplin spoke of *Limelight* as though this was to be the great achievement of his life. I was to discover that he felt similarly about each new work he conceived. He again and again spoke of his London childhood. He described the London parks that I enjoyed as places of desolation and despair, when he knew them fit only for the lonely and the destitute. Oddly he seemed to be longing with passion for a London that had hurt and horrified him, a London that from his description I hadn't known at all.

The cast of *Limelight* was to include every available member of his family. His son Sydney was to play a young composer; another son, Charlie junior, and his half-brother, Wheeler Dryden, were to appear in a ballet sequence; even his three small children, Geraldine, Michael, and Josephine, were to appear briefly as neighbourhood waifs. Hearing of the place the children held in this privileged and protected world, I came up effortlessly with another role for myself: *Daughter of a genius.* Without regret I abandoned what little loyalty I had left for the natural father who had disappointed me, and adopted, on the spot, the father I felt I'd had every right to expect: a father brilliant, worldly, charming, handsome, rich, and strong.

I spent half the night sitting up with my mother at the Beverly Hills Hotel, telling her everything I'd seen and heard, failing only to enlighten her about the enhancing of our family circle.

The next day I was taken to see the Chaplin studios and to meet the cameraman and crew. Although located in Hollywood proper, his studios were as different in setting as they were in spirit from the others. Rows of mock Tudor cottages flanked the gate, and stretching off to one side was a large, beautiful orange grove, a corner of the pastoral California still untouched from the days of his first triumphs. Just as he was nostalgic for the squalor of a vanished London, so was he nostalgic for the physical charm of early Hollywood, when, according to Chaplin, it was a small village with a fine climate, the air scented with orange blossoms, and the view of the Hollywood hills clear and unblemished by smog. A supermarket now stands on the site of the orange grove, and after he was expelled from America Chaplin's studios passed into the hands of Herb Alpert and his Tijuana Brass. One needn't be a full-blown nostalgist like Chaplin to appreciate the difference.

I met Chaplin later that day at Brooks, the costumiers, and he repeated with even greater precision the instructions he had given for outfitting me for the test. "My mother," he said, "used to wear a loose knitted cardigan, a blouse with a high neck and a little bow, and a worn velvet jacket." We consulted *Punch* magazines of the period to be certain that no detail was wrong. Again I saw how intent he was upon recapturing the past in this film: the dressing rooms, the boarding houses, the agents' offices, the pubs, all the melancholy landmarks of his lonely apprenticeship. "Melancholy" was a word he was to use frequently when speaking of his plans for *Limelight.*

My mother, in the meantime, had found a moderately priced apartment to rent for our stay, and the next day, when my schedule of classes and rehearsals began, she moved us out of the Beverly Hills Hotel into a Hollywood-style hacienda, complete with patio and fountain, that we both thought "romantic."

The weather was always fine and so we rehearsed in the garden of their house, Chaplin, Jerry Epstein, and I. Chaplin was the same director he'd been at the screen test: he told me what to do, I did it. He was never in repose for a moment, always moving, demonstrating a gesture, setting a scene, explaining a shot, always trying to make me aware of (so that in the end I would take for granted) the nearness of the camera. He asked for certain effects that to me seemed raw and naive and outdated

But they were his style, as much a part of the performer as his cane and his bowler, and now he expected these effects from me. Willing and eager—and adoring—I gave myself over to them and to him. I saw how clear to him was every nuance of the performance as it would register on the movie screen. Nothing was left to chance. There was no such thing as chance. There was only his genius.

Sometimes he would relent about our diet and we would break the rehearsal for cottage cheese or yogurt. The rehearsals were intense and there were days when deliberately to break the spell—days when our work had gone very well or very poorly—Chaplin took the three of us and Oona off to the Farmers' Market in downtown Hollywood. There was superb local produce for sale there, and open-air stalls where you could buy every conceivable kind of specialty to eat on the spot. I remember distinctly Chaplin buying a small slice of pâté that cost exactly eighteen dollars. They wrapped the pâté in silver paper and he gave them one ten, one five, and three singles. Oona says that my standard of living changed from that day on.

I awoke each morning in a state of joy. There was the sun out the window. There was my mother, entirely to myself. There was the great film genius opposite whom I was playing a leading role in his new film. And here was I: young, pretty, slightly in love with Sydney—or was it Charlie?—Chaplin.

Melissa Hayden and André Eglevsky came from New York to rehearse the ballet sequence. Melissa, a superb dancer trained by Balanchine and a celebrated leading ballerina with the New York City Ballet, was to double for me as the dancer. I was required to attend all the rehearsals, and when the camera was close enough to permit me to do so, to wheel into frame and out as fast as possible—whereupon Melissa would take over again. The effect was so convincing that for years afterward I was complimented on my dancing. However, it was during one of those dance rehearsals that I thought momentarily the miracle had run its course. One morning after our exercise class, Oona and I wandered onto the sound stage to watch Hayden and Eglevsky rehearsing. Trying to create as little disturbance as possible, we silently dropped into the nearest chairs, failing to notice the huge mirror that was balanced up against the chairbacks. As I leaned over to whisper something to Oona, the mirror crashed to the floor. Chaplin turned to me, all his fury registering without the aid of a single syllable. I knew from things he'd already said at rehearsals how deeply rooted in him were all the theatrical superstitions—and this, of course, was the worst omen of all, a mirror breaking just at the start of a new undertaking. I would be driven off the set and sent packing to England—it had all been too good to be true. But after a long pause—during which he glared and I shook—he gave a sign for the rehearsal to continue. The clumsy novice was to be given another chance.

In the evenings, when I wasn't studying my lines or we hadn't been invited to the Chaplins' for dinner, my mother and I would walk down to Hollywood Boulevard. The shops seemed always to be open, the movie theatres alight, and after we had picked through the glittery junk jewellery for sale along the way, we would sit in the window seats at Musso Franks, an old-fashioned restaurant

that Chaplin had known when he first arrived in Hollywood, and to which he'd introduced us. Out on the street
you could see all the hopefuls parading by, would-be stars
of all ages and descriptions, checking their reflections in
every window, checking out one another, waiting with
patient desperation to be discovered. I, who had been discovered, was hypnotised by the grotesque extremes to
which the desire for stardom could carry people. Those
nights, looking out from our window seats at Musso
Franks, did nothing to diminish the sensation I had frequently in California of living in a dream.

On most Saturday nights, the Chaplins invited friends
to join them for dinner. There I met the writer James Agee,
deeply shy, always agonisingly self-conscious before he
could wrench words free. I met Clifford Odets, a forceful,
furious, dictatorial man, who much later became a dear
friend. I met William Saroyan, then married to Oona's
girlhood friend Carol Marcus, and about whom I only
remember the beautiful liquidity of his eyes. By a few
years I had missed meeting there the refugee artists who'd
come to settle in California in the thirties—Thomas Mann,
Hanns Eisler, and Bertolt Brecht. It was the era of the
political witchhunt, and everyone in the room seemed to
have been touched somehow by the anti-Communist cru-
sade that would result in the destruction of many careers
and many lives, in Hollywood particularly. The conversation was mainly about politics, though at some point in
the evening, Chaplin would invariably launch into the
story of *Limelight*. But it was mostly for himself to hear
the story—to evaluate it, to savour it, to refine it—rather

than for the pleasure of his guests, most of whom had heard it more than once before.

Here is the story.

Calvero, a once-famous, aging music hall comedian, has through drink come to be living in a cheap boarding house in Edwardian London. One day, unemployed and a little tight, he comes into the hallway and smells gas coming from a nearby room. The door is locked and when he breaks it in he discovers a young girl stretched out on the bed, very close to dying. She is Theresa, who has kept to herself after renting a room there, and whom Calvero has not seen before. He carries her to his room, and when the landlady finds her there and threatens to throw her into the street, Calvero promises that he will look after her and nurse her back to health.

But when Theresa is conscious she says she has no desire to go on living. She reveals to Calvero that she had been a promising dancer, but a terrible shock—she had seen her sister walking the streets—has caused her to lose the use of her lower limbs. Calvero tells her about his past successes in the music halls, a story interspersed with dream-scenes of his triumphs, some of which wishfully include a healthy and happy Theresa. Calvero wins her confidence (and her love) and she begins to recover health and happiness. After Calvero has encouraged her and bullied her like the best of fathers, she discovers she can walk again.

She sets out now to resume her ballet career, Calvero sets out to resume his as a comic. He visits agents' offices, but though all know him and admire him, no one will hire him because of his drinking. Eventually he is given a few pennies to perform at a third-rate theatre, but the house is nearly empty and he is a dismal failure; he returns to the bottle. Theresa, on the other hand, has auditioned for the prestigious Empire Theatre Ballet and won the leading role in their new production. The composer falls in love with her, and she with him, though it is Calvero she still hopes to marry. Calvero doesn't want her to sacrifice her successful young man for a failure like himself, and just as Theresa is becoming the toast of London, he disappears. Over the years Theresa's stardom grows, but she never stops searching for Calvero. Finally she discovers him busking in a London pub. Now it is she who insists on taking him home with her, and soon she is able to arrange with her producer a benefit performance for him at the Empire. All the stars of London will perform, and she herself will dance. This, she tells him, will be the beginning of his comeback.

The great night arrives. *Tout Londres* is there. Even the young composer, now a great man himself, is present to lend moral support. And Calvero is once more a triumph. He performs a hilarious act with another comedian, at the climax of which he falls, as planned, into a drum in the orchestra pit. The audience applauds wildly, but Calvero has done serious injury to his back, or his heart, or both. He is carried offstage in the drum, to where Theresa, most distraught, is waiting for him in the wings. Despite his protestations to the contrary, she realizes that the injury is not feigned or part of the act, but she is called immediately onstage to perform the ballet. There in the wings Calvero dies, while Theresa, young and radiant, pirouettes unknowingly into the future. THE END.

The summary he gave at those Saturday evening dinners obviously couldn't begin to suggest the merciless hold that Chaplin's story would have upon an audience's feelings. What the story pointed to, told at the dinner table, was sentimentality—what Chaplin brought to the screen was passionate emotion. Deepening a conventional Victorian melodrama into his own kind of expressive art, he resembled, of course, his great literary idol, Charles Dickens, with whom he shared a strong autobiographical interest in scenarios of abysmal disaster and miraculous recovery. And *Limelight,* with its devotion to the London period atmosphere, was to be the most openly Dickensian of all his works. The backstage world provided him with seediness and with glamour—most important of all for Chaplin, with an ideal setting to dramatise the wrenching fickleness of fortune: star one day, failure the next. Into the music hall environment of his early manhood he would bring, in still another incarnation, those two characters from earliest childhood that his imagination could never abandon: the defeated father, the unbalanced mother. In *Limelight* they would become the drunken, down-and-out Calvero, and the crippled dancer, Theresa—she just one in the line of damaged heroines inspired by the memory of his mother, heroines extending from the blind flower-seller of *City Lights* to the penniless waif of *Modern Times* and the young female ex-con of *Monsieur Verdoux.* I think that what particularly excited Chaplin about the *Limelight* story was that at long last the damaged girl was to develop into a mature woman, strong, independent, completely in command of her powers. What would make the film so passionate was just this celebration of a young woman's triumphal recovery, a celebration tempered of course by the seemingly sacrificial death of the music hall comedian. Recounting the story of *Limelight* to his dinner guests Saturday after Saturday seemed to provide Chaplin not just with the thrilling expectation of a new film achievement, but with something almost like the satisfaction of reaching back into the London of 1914 to rescue the mother once and for all from the blight of mental disease. Only years afterward, when I came to know Chaplin as "Charlie" and to stay regularly with him and Oona and the children in their house above Lake Geneva, did I realize how much the example of Oona—of her loving devotion and her quiet strength—was responsible for finally erasing the image of broken womanhood that his mother's suffering had imprinted on his artistic conscience.

To ease me into the filming, we began with the scene in Calvero's room, where I was required merely to lie in a coma. However, the first three days' filming had to be scrapped because Chaplin was dissatisfied with the camera work of his old associate Rollie Totheroh. He then engaged Karl Struss, a more up-to-date technician, to replace Totheroh, and this cast a gloom over the set. Totheroh had shot most of Chaplin's earlier films and, as he was no longer young, it was clear that this was probably the last job of his career—a Calvero winding up in the drum. But Chaplin, generous and loyal as he could be in pensioning his workers, was utterly ruthless when it came to the standards he'd set for his film. To me what all this meant was that I had to wait another week before I could begin to show Chaplin, and the world, what I could do.

When we did begin, all that meticulous rehearsing paid off—we played beautifully together. He was happy with me and I was thrilled. But then came the true test: we moved from the simple dialogues to the scene where Theresa discovers (hysterically) that she can walk again. As a young actress I had difficulty in weeping and I dreaded the scene. I knew that the tears wouldn't come when needed. The morning of the shooting, at the height of my panic, I was summoned to Chaplin's dressing room. He said he wanted to go over the scene purely for the moves and the words. "I want no emotion. Save that for the floor." I obeyed. Suddenly Chaplin was furious with me, as though I'd shattered a second mirror. "But, Mr. Chaplin," I weakly protested, "I thought that was what you wanted—just a technical run-through of the scene." This remark drove Chaplin into a greater fury. "There is no such thing as technical acting, only bad acting!" I started to weep, and was steered by him onto the floor, where the crew, notified beforehand of his plan, were ready to begin filming immediately. We shot the scene in one take. Chaplin had judged perfectly what would do the job— rather like Calvero understanding what magic would be required to make Theresa walk again.

I should add that the exacting, dictatorial ingenuity that worked like a charm on me, an adoring surrogate daughter, had a rather different effect on his real son, Sydney. Before the filming had begun, Sydney Chaplin had taken me for a romantic tête-à-tête at the Cock and Bull, a Hollywood version of an English pub that served roast beef with crumpets and raspberry jam on the side. There he had been wickedly funny about his strong-minded father's eccentricities—as sons can be about strong-minded fathers under the sign of the Cock and Bull. But once Sydney reported to begin his role in the film, he lacked all defensive wit, and confronted with those paternal "eccentricities," became nervous and wooden on the set. It was only when he appeared in *Funny Girl* on the New York stage some years later that Sydney's considerable sexual charm—which one sees just a touch of in *Limelight*— was able to make its way fully into his performance.

By the Christmas break, the important scenes had nearly been completed. Only the music hall and the ballet sequences remained to be shot, and my responsibility to the film was almost over. I began to feel the panic of the actor who is nearing the end of a long and secure employment, added to which there was the strangeness of being alone with my mother and away from home over Christmas. John was in his boarding school in England. He wrote that he was happy and not lonely, but I still suspected myself of extreme selfishness for taking my mother off for so long. It was curious to see the streets decorated with white cardboard trees and papier-mâché reindeer, and the tinsel aglitter in the sun. We were asked to join the Chaplins for Christmas day, but no amount of kindness lessened the feeling of dislocation I knew my mother was sharing with me. I was nearly twenty-one and felt as homesick as a child.

We recommenced filming after the holiday, and I found myself growing more and more unhappy with the sense of things winding down. The ballet was shot in a reconstruction of an Edwardian theatre, and I watched from the stalls while Chaplin turned all his interest toward

Melissa Hayden. To my mortification, I rediscovered the same feelings I had had when my father would show his preference for my lively and charming cousin Erica over me, so serious and uncertain. Melissa was playful and flirtatious with Chaplin and he responded with pleasure. Had I not been so polite and respectful, I realised, I would have pleased him more. Too late now. Wracked by these vain and dismal thoughts, I was spied by Nigel Bruce, who was also appearing in the film. As only an Englishman can, he boomed out in a huge voice, "What are you doing, sitting in the corner like a little mouse?" This urgent question was leaked to that vampire, the British tabloid press, who immediately labelled me "The Little Mouse," a name which infuriated me for years whenever it cropped up in one *Daily Beast* or another.

After the ballet sequence, Chaplin and I performed a gentle patter scene together, to this day my favourite scene in the film. He was costumed nearly to resemble his old character, the Tramp, and I wore a large pink bonnet and a matching frilly tutu-like dress. All the scene consisted of was a slightly incoherent question and answer routine, and a few gentle dance steps together; nonetheless, I was strongly moved to think that this must reach back to his earliest memories of the Edwardian music hall—moved too by the connection between my role in the scene and those young and unobtainable girls he adored while still a young performer on the London stage. It seemed to me, even while playing the scene, that more was crystallised for him in this scene than any audience would ever realise, including even the feelings of incredulity and loss he had suffered when his pretty, young mother had be-

come insane and disappeared into an asylum. This was
the sweet and easy way it was supposed to have been,
but alas, could only be in a sketch with a bonneted young
innocent on a music hall stage.

The arrival of Buster Keaton was greatly anticipated
by us all. He hadn't been in films for many years and
was to appear with Chaplin in the final theatre sequence—
Keaton as a nearsighted and cracked professor of the key-
board, Chaplin as an inspired and cracked violinist. Keaton
was fifty-six when he made *Limelight*, but gave the impression of having suffered through a life twice that long.
From his lined face and grave expression one would have
thought that he had neither known a lighthearted moment
nor was able to instigate one. His reserve was extreme,
as was his isolation. He remained to himself on the set,
until one day, to my astonishment, he took from his pocket
a colour postcard of a large Hollywood mansion and
showed it to me. It was the sort of postcard that tourists
pick up in Hollywood drugstores. In the friendliest, most
intimate way, he explained to me that it had once been
his home. That was it. He retreated back into silence and
never addressed a word to me again. In his scene with
Chaplin, however, he was brilliantly alive with invention.
Some of his gags may even have been a little too incandes-
cent for Chaplin, because, laugh as he did at the rushes
in the screening room, Chaplin didn't see fit to allow them
all into the final version of the film.

I hoped each day not to be told that I was free to
go home. I knew that my mother longed to get back to
her own life, particularly to my brother John, but I was
determined to hold on to *Limelight* until the last moment.

My dismissal came in a phone call from the production office of the Chaplin studios. I would be given two weeks more of expense money in case I was needed for any looping or stills, but on the books my job was over. When they asked what arrangements we wished made for our return to England, it felt to me not as though it were a company that was letting me go, but the new family I had adopted. I dreaded our departure, even though Chaplin promised to come to London for the premiere, and Sydney promised to come to London for me. On February 9 my mother and I boarded the train to begin the journey home. We had been in America just over four months.

The London we were returning to was still suffering a postwar spiritual recession and seemed to me particularly drab and insular after the affluence and liveliness I'd seen in America. Apart from the few films produced by Alexander Korda, the film industry was extremely provincial. The theatre was deadly. It was still some years before the emergence of Pinter, Arden, Osborne, Wesker, Storey, and Mercer; and further down the line, David Hare and Christopher Hampton. For the most part the West End survived on stylish revivals of *Lady Windermere's Fan* and middlebrow domestic drama. The Festival Hall was beginning to be built on the South Bank and there had been some theatrical stirrings at the "Festival of Britain," but my first impulse upon returning was to run right back where I'd come from. My contemporaries Jean Simmons and Audrey Hepburn had done just that, and following the example of Deborah Kerr, England's first postwar actress to become an international film star, were in Hollywood for good. But however much I now wanted a career in films, I wanted above all to build a stage career, and the place to do that was London. As yet the only British actress who had managed to be recognised both on the London stage and in American films was Vivien Leigh, and her example didn't inspire confidence since she was never accorded by the theatrical Establishment the esteem she deserved as an English stage actress precisely because of the reputation she had made abroad as a beautiful film star.

Of my own generation of actresses born in the thirties, only Dorothy Tutin had begun to achieve recognition on the stage. In less than a decade it was to be a most remarkable generation of actresses: Eileen Atkins, Jill Bennett, Judi Dench, Rosemary Harris, Glenda Jackson, Natasha Parry, Joan Plowright, Vanessa Redgrave, Maggie Smith, Janet Suzman, Mary Ure, Billie Whitelaw. But at this time they were all sensibly learning their craft in good repertory companies far from London, and for better or worse, I was out there on my own, and I found it, when I got home, a tough place to be.

Despite the publicity I had already received as Chaplin's ingenue, I would still be an unknown until *Limelight* was released, and no one appeared to be hurrying to get hold of me before I was hot. Not only were there no film offers, but on the first morning home I found a telegram under the door informing me that the stage production of *Richard II*, to which I'd thought I was returning, had been cancelled. What sharpened the disappointment was that only a few weeks earlier, on the way through New York, I had discouraged two Broadway producers from offering me roles, one as the heroine in Giraudoux's *Ondine*, preferring to do Shakespeare in England instead.

Relations with young men, always difficult for me, became even worse as they treated the young woman they had read about in the newspapers with an alarming respectfulness that kindled all my stiff and self-conscious propriety. Although I sometimes yearned for Sydney Chaplin's arrival in London, I was mostly content that he should stay where he was so I could get on with becoming a famous actress. But then becoming a famous actress was what was causing me such trouble with the young men, and even with my only friend, Heather Stannard. The development of our two budding careers had till then paralleled each other, but now, just as I was getting all this publicity, she had hit a difficult period. She was touring in an indifferent revival of a Noel Coward play, and hard as I tried I couldn't stop myself from talking obsessively, to her or anyone else who would listen, about the thrill of working with Chaplin and the trial of waiting for the film to appear. So that friendship, once so easy, became strained as well. Only to my Aunt Mary could I speak with complete candour about what had happened to me as an actress in California and what I wanted now.

It was June, we had returned in February, and the money put aside from the film began dwindling, for all that it had sounded like a fortune to us when I was first offered the role. Broadcasting for the BBC was still a source of a little income—and of pleasure—and fortunately, the poet and playwright James Forsyth at this time came up with a radio play in verse, *Adelaise,* which he had written for me. It was fortunate not only because it provided work and a salary, but because one day at lunch in the BBC canteen, Forsyth told me that the director of the Old Vic was searching for a young actress to appear in their new production of *Romeo and Juliet*. Would I like him to suggest me for the role? I had been playing Juliet for the family since I saw Norma Shearer in the film when I was seven, and playing Juliet for auditions since I was twelve; I said yes.

It happened as simply as that—as simply as the telegram had come from Chaplin asking for my photograph. The irony has always been that however hard I have pursued my career, then or now, the roles meaning most to me have seemingly fallen from nowhere. Probably I could have saved myself a lot of wear and tear had I all along followed my impulses and sat off in a corner somewhere quietly reading until they came to drag me on the stage in costume. I think that few professions—from the beginning of a career until the end—have so much to do with chance and so little to do with the calculations of will.

I was up all night deciding which speech would be the most stunning for my audition, but when I saw the director, Hugh Hunt, that next evening at his office above the Old Vic Theatre off the Waterloo Road, he treated me as someone who no longer needed to read for a role— he said he had admired me since *Ring Round the Moon* and wanted me for Juliet. We would begin to rehearse in five weeks: Alan Badel was to play Romeo, Peter Finch Mercutio, Athene Seyler the Nurse, and Sir Lewis Casson Friar Laurence. Hunt would direct, and Roger Furse, who had designed the film of Olivier's *Hamlet*, would do the sets and costumes. I realised on the way home that it was the first time in England that I had been regarded as an established professional actress instead of as this child who acted.

The Old Vic was first launched as the Royal Victoria Theatre in 1880 by Emma Cons, a devoted churchwoman who hoped to save the working class from the iniquitous depravities of Victorian music halls by serving them tea and serious entertainment. Set in a working-class district just off Waterloo Road, the theatre had none of the elegance or grandeur of Vienna's Burgtheater or the Comédie Française. Nevertheless, until the nineteen sixties, it was the nearest thing England had to a national theatre and the only theatre in London where the best classical drama was regularly performed. Beneath its unexciting façade of good clean British worthiness was an institution of extraordinary artistic achievement, where Olivier, Gielgud, Richardson, Edith Evans, and Peggy Ashcroft had all performed their great roles. Unlike the more rigidly traditional Comédie Française, there was no prescribed style of acting handed on from one generation to the next—simply a tradition of individual excellence that could be bent to suit a strong new approach to production or acting. In 1933 Peggy Ashcroft had performed a greatly acclaimed Juliet at the Old Vic, one that I had heard about all my life.

The only *Romeo and Juliet* I'd seen on the stage was the Peter Brook production I'd auditioned for when I was fourteen. However, I had already read all I could about the actresses who had played Juliet in the past, in particular about Fanny Kemble, who at the age of twenty, in 1830, had made her Covent Garden debut in the role. It was heartening to know that she had felt herself then utterly lacking in stagecraft, and had to make do with a display of her own emotional apparatus, such as it was. And it was something of a relief to know that she had been a year younger than I, for I was to be the youngest actress to play Juliet since the war. I realised that one could come under fire on the matter of age alone. "Is she mature enough to play a fourteen-year-old?" Fortunately Peter Brook's production seven years earlier had added greatly to the credibility of the play by casting all the younger parts with more youthful actors than was conventional then—a fact which may have helped draw Hunt to me.

I studied Ellen Terry's *Lectures on Shakespeare's Women*, read the preface to the play by Harley Granville-Barker, and I went to the public library and had a good time working through the Furness Variorum. I made my notes, studied my books, and then I went off by myself for a week to Warwickshire, to the village of Headlington near Stratford-upon-Avon. Paul Scofield had told me of a Tudor cottage where he had stayed while playing at Stratford, and I'd written to the landlady and taken a room for a week. I forgot the whole mass of criticism and scholarship I had dutifully waded through and spent a week alone— my first solitary holiday ever—taking long walks and reciting my lines. I didn't have to memorise them, only to brush up on what I'd learned fourteen years before.

As for the research, it had stilled my conscience, if nothing more. I had done everything in my power to *understand* the play and the role, though I'd realized all along that Juliet is not a complicated character like Lady Macbeth, whose motives gradually become uncertain and unknown, even to herself; she is a young girl with clear and graspable intentions, a girl of great courage and high birth, and all the recklessness of a spoiled and adored child. Her father confessor, Friar Laurence, again and again warns her to be patient, but in adversity, after Romeo's banishment, she becomes a most determined young woman, her resolution never faltering, save for one terrifying moment before she drinks the potion that might lead rather to her death than to an awakening in Romeo's arms. Determination never wavers, not even when she awakens in the tomb to find Romeo dead, and takes her own life. None of the footnotes I'd read was going to help me to convey the sense of emotional abandonment and the strength of purpose that separates her halfway through the play from the wilful child she'd been.

On the first day of rehearsal, I took the bus to Waterloo Road intimidated not at all by the thought of reading through the play, which I could hardly wait to do, but at meeting the cast. I had seen Alan Badel as a brilliant Richard III at the Birmingham Repertory Theatre when I was on tour with *The Lady's Not for Burning.* I had seen Peter Finch in the leading role opposite Dame Edith Evans in James Bridie's *Daphne Laureola,* and Sir Lewis Casson and Athene Seyler were distinguished members of the profession. I was accustomed by now to being the youngest member of a theatrical company, but not of simultaneously being leading lady. I hoped I wouldn't be resented because of my age, or that it wouldn't appear to everyone that I had been asked to play Juliet only because of Charlie Chaplin.

My youthful egoism had failed to inform me that at the first reading of a play, no actor, no matter how old or experienced, is overcome with confidence. The last thing anyone aside from me had it in mind to worry about was whether I was twenty or a hundred, nor did it turn out that the name "Charlie Chaplin" was on everyone's lips.

We were to form a circle for the reading, and I seated myself between the two attractive leading men. Hugh Hunt read us an essay he'd written about the play, but I couldn't hear it as I'd become temporarily deaf from terror. But when the reading began I could speak as well as hear, and it soon became evident to all of us that there was vitality in the ensemble and that something original might come of it. Right off, Alan Badel and I sensed we were a good match. Half French, with Italianate good looks, he conformed to my idea of a dark, volatile, delicate Romeo. I developed a crush on him before the reading was over, which, given the play, probably didn't hurt my performance.

At the beginning of rehearsals I naturally found easiest the earlier, girlish scenes. The balcony scene was fine from the first day we went through it, with me standing on a rickety table to remind us of the physical distance separating the lovers. The early scenes with the Nurse went as easily as if we were playing in a nursery, but then we came to the banishment scene, in which Juliet is told by the Nurse that on the very day she has celebrated her secret wedding, Romeo has killed her cousin Tybalt and been banished for it to Verona. I did the scene and nothing happened. I manufactured a "tragic" response that had nothing to do with Juliet or with me. Hugh Hunt, who all along had treated me as he had the first evening I came to meet him—as an established, professional actress—qui-

etly told me that the scene was "not very good." "I know
it isn't," I answered, but was at a loss as to what to do.
What was worse, my performance was so wooden and
dry that Athene Seyler, as the Nurse, had been affected
by it and couldn't find her way into the scene either. I
continued like that, and came to dread the run-throughs
of the play; I would slink off into the wings immediately
afterward. Not until the last complete run-through in London, when I was carried away by the sheer narrative excitement of the story, did I all at once stop reaching for an
effect, and let the moving dramatic facts of the case effortlessly, as it were, do the acting for me. And forever after
it was always the same in any play I did: the dangerously
difficult scenes would provoke at first an artificial appropriate-
ness, and only when I had come to feel them in their necessary
relationship to what came before and after could I penetrate
the theatrical response to one of my own.

We were to open the production at the Edinburgh
Festival in mid-August and after three weeks there transfer
to the Old Vic. On October 16, a month after the Old
Vic opening of *Romeo and Juliet*, *Limelight* was to premiere
in London at the Odeon Leicester Square and a week later
in New York at the Astor and the Trans-Lux. The immediate result of my burgeoning anticipation was a painful
carbuncle that developed under my arm and almost prevented me from joining the Old Vic company in Edinburgh. Once there, I came down with a monumental cold.
It only remained to see what would afflict me on opening
night.

I settled into a small boarding house rather than spend
half my salary on one of Edinburgh's hotels, and there

the landlady insisted I go straight to bed. She brought me, as a cure-all, a glass of hot green ginger wine mixed with an equal amount of Scotch whisky. I went to sleep blind drunk and awoke the next morning as healthy as the landlady had promised, to be given a huge breakfast in bed. All this for three pounds a week.

We played in the Assembly Rooms, where generations of Scottish Presbyterian ministers had convened for ecclesiastical business. As the hall had a platform that could double as a thrust stage, it was used during festival time as a theatre. Outside, a statue of John Knox pointed a finger toward heaven, bidding us forsake all earthly delights, and within the walls were hung with portraits of dour clerical worthies; nonetheless, our production was never so spirited in London as it was during those three weeks in Edinburgh. It may have had as much to do with the intimacy created with the audience by the thrust stage as with our freshness. The opening night was as successful as any I've ever known. No carbuncle, no cold, no deafness, no headache—just the extraordinarily rare sense that I had fulfilled the role I'd been rehearsing now for two-thirds of my life.

A week later my mother arrived by train with my cousin Norma. I had been allowed to settle into the role before my mother's arrival. My sternest critic, alert to all my faults and mannerisms, she would never fail to point them out to me, simply and accurately. This time she pronounced herself "satisfied," but gave me several strong notes anyway. I resented them bitterly, saw that they were right, and changed my performance accordingly.

I arrived back in London on a Sunday afternoon and

found a letter from Oona saying that she and Mr. Chaplin would be arriving in two weeks to prepare for the premiere of *Limelight*. There was also a telegram from Sydney Chaplin. I had heard little from him in the six months since I'd left California, but now he wanted to know if I would like him to come to England for the first night of *Romeo and Juliet*. I was frightened of any distraction that would prevent me from concentrating totally on the performance the following Thursday. I had no idea how I would handle a suitor if he arrived at any time, let alone at that moment. However much I may have encouraged Sydney's attentions, I knew I had been drawn more to the idea of being Chaplin's daughter-in-law than being Sydney's wife. But I didn't have the wherewithal to say no and Sydney arrived in time to accompany my mother to the opening.

When the tabloids learned that *Romeo* and *Limelight* were to open within a month of each other with an all-but-unknown young woman in starring roles, the publicity began. Most of it seemed to me to place an alarmingly mistaken emphasis on what was happening. When I read stories headlined "Will She Make It?" and "Her Big Test," I could only go to sleep at night mumbling, "No, she won't," and "Test failed."

On the morning of the opening, I felt the beginning of that numbing depression I had already come to associate with first nights. I knew what effect it might have on my performance if it got out of control: I could lose all spontaneity and stand outside myself like my own most hostile critic, judging my every utterance with cold contempt. What "stage fright" means to me is just this sense of separation between actress and self. I am isolated from

her, she is isolated from me, and both of us are isolated
from the role. It can be an experience of the most terrifying
fragmentation.

Monday, Sept. 15, 1952

Rested from two until four. Then tea, boiled egg, toast,
with plenty of honey for energy. Bathed and dressed. Taxi
to the theatre. Dressing room full of flowers. Telegrams
piled on makeup table. Can't resist taking time to open
every one and seeing who has sent flowers. Rush around
to the stage door to see if I can find suitable containers.
Now thirty minutes behind my scheduled preparation
time. Put on dressing gown, turn out lights, lie on floor
for ten minutes to calm down. Guilty about running
around using energy I might better store up for the play.
My dresser brings in a cup of coffee. I start to make up.
Much calmer now. Even begin to feel a touch of anticipation. Try not to worry about whether I will perform as
well as in Edinburgh. Try not to worry about the difficult
scenes. Too late for that. Makeup and hair completed.
Three quarters of an hour to go before curtain rises at
seven-thirty. I go to Athene Seyler's dressing room. We
embrace and wish each other luck. Then Alan Badel, Peter
Finch, and Sir Lewis. Back to my own room where I firmly
close the door and start to hum vocal exercises for resonance. Am calm enough for a moment to realise that my
mother will be even more nervous out front than I will
be on the stage. Half an hour before performance is announced over my loud speaker, I hear through the speaker
first sounds of audience arriving. Try to empty my mind.
Try to relax by deep and steady breathing. Marie Antoin-

ette on the way to the guillotine must have felt the same: let's just get there and get it over with. The quarter of an hour is called and my dresser comes in to put me into the opening costume. Five minutes to curtain and the actors who begin the play are summoned to the stage. Silence. The audience is rising to their feet. The opening bars of the national anthem. A murmuring as they take their seats again. Then silence. I know the house lights have gone to half, then to black. The opening music for *Romeo and Juliet*. The curtain rises, the audience applauds the set, the Duke of Verona speaks. It is happening. I feel slightly sick and have to remind myself just how many years I have wanted this. I want to weep and go home. I go into the wings and find a chair behind a flat where I cannot be seen. I sit quietly, my hands folded in my lap. Suddenly I feel very young, almost childlike, and extremely calm. I hear the Nurse and Lady Capulet beginning our scene. I hear my cue. I have to force myself into action as though I am to plunge into a freezing sea. I run across the stage toward my mother and my nurse. I am distracted for a moment by the brief applause that greets my appearance, then everything begins to fade except the reality of the play. I feel that I have a wonderful story to tell.

Had I kept a journal at the time, my notes would have resembled these. It is more or less a record of any opening night, with the exception that Juliet was for me, as it is for many classical actresses, the greatest test of my early career. The problem of the opening night remains always, and that is to transform the anxiety into energy and the energy into identification with the role. It is not a matter of learning over the years to shake off tension, but of learning to bear the tension until it is at its strongest and one is self-propelled onto the stage like an arrow that flies straight and true.

Alan Badel and I lay dead in each other's arms in the tomb of the Capulets. Our part in the play was over. I listened to the closing couplet that had echoed through my childhood.

> For never was a story of more woe,
> Than this of Juliet and her Romeo.

A solemn roll of drums, the curtain fell, and we scrambled to our feet to join the other members of the company for the curtain call. The principal actors stepped forward in turn; my moment arrived, I bowed to the audience, and when I turned to rejoin the company, I found the cast on stage was applauding me as well. We took fourteen more calls—so it was reported in the newspapers the next day. I began to think it was just possible that we were a success, insofar as I was able to think. Friends came round to congratulate me, including new friends whom until then I had only known as celebrated names in the theatre. My mother appeared, looking as beautiful as she had one night in Bristol, when, wearing a black chiffon dress and a white gardenia in her hair, she came to kiss me goodnight before leaving for a party. She said that she had been so terrified before the curtain rose that her entire row of stalls had shaken with her. She told me I had given a beautiful performance, but she had some notes to give me the next day. My Aunt Mary and cousin Norma were in the audience, and Mary told me that all her hopes for me had been fulfilled that night.

I awoke long before daybreak the next morning and had to wait nearly four hours before I could rush out to the newsagents to buy the papers. In general the reviews were extremely good, although Kenneth Tynan's in the *Evening Standard*—the best for me personally—wasn't to appear until the end of the week. An obedient child of the theatrical world, I pondered long and deep over the truths hidden in these five-hundred-word notices written at midnight in under an hour, devastated by so little as a nasty epithet, elated beyond measure by a word of praise. But even I began to lose my naive and supersensitive idealism that next morning, when I read reviews in two leading papers, one of which complimented me on the clear and lyrical way I spoke the poetry but regretted that I didn't as yet fully comprehend Juliet's tragic dilemma, while the other applauded me for my passionate involvement in the drama and my persuasive creation of character but lamented my inability to speak blank verse. The fact is that nothing I have read in newspaper notices has ever led me to reconsider speaking a line, let alone reinterpret a role. The reason is simple, and has little to do with arrogance. It is that the alternatives presented even by the most imaginative of reviewers—and they are never in great supply; the history of newspaper reviewing is not a glorious one—constitute about one percent of the alternatives that have been tried and considered and rejected by the actor during the course of four to six weeks of rehearsal. Taste and judgement is so at the heart of acting that, rightly or wrongly, the actor can only feel it an enormous presumption on the part of any critic to assume the role of final arbiter. The purpose of the critical notice is to form the judgement of the audience and not to educate the actor, who is of necessity a better student of his gifts and certainly of his weaknesses than someone who sees him work for two hours once a year.

I could hardly wait that second evening to get back to the theatre and perform without the extraneous pressures and distractions of the preceding weeks. The press had other plans for me. In November, *Time* was to publish a cover story about the new young star of *Limelight* and *Romeo and Juliet;* the magazine's reporters had begun interviewing my family, my friends, and just about any actor who had ever appeared with me anywhere. To be the subject of a big story in a big magazine seemed to me thrilling, yet I was disturbed by the thought of strangers looking into my private life, particularly the sensitive, distressing business of my parents' divorce. Then too, from out of the bowels of the *Daily Beast,* a new epithet was delivered forth to describe (and annoy) the quintessential me: to replace "The Little Mouse," "The English Rose." What irritated me about the label was being stuck with a label, any label, virtually before I'd begun. I wasn't a flower; I was an actress who could *pretend* to be a flower. So I remember protesting to my mother, who told me to quiet down and enjoy it.

Mainly that was what I did. I read the headlines and looked at my photographs and had the time of my life. "Juliet at Last." "Juliet Charms London." And then Kenneth Tynan's review, calling me the best Juliet he had ever seen. Sydney Chaplin, who had seen me last in Hollywood addressing his father as "Mr. Chaplin," was stunned somewhat, when he came round, to find in place of the little mouse a creature of enormous confidence and frighteningly high spirits. That is, when he could find me. I was either at the theatre or getting ready to go there— eating my solitary meal at an odd hour, resting on my bed for my performance at night. I had no time from playing Juliet for having a real romance, and indeed, it was not until the following year that I had my first complete sexual relationship. Crushes on leading men seemed to content me, and Sydney had now been replaced by Romeo himself. Gradually Sydney faded from my life, certainly to my regret, possibly to his.

Headlines in the morning papers only a few days later reported that Chaplin's reentry permit to the United States had been withdrawn, even while he was on a transatlantic ship heading for London and for the *Limelight* opening. On leaving New York with Oona and their four children, he had been careful to receive reassurances from the U.S. Immigration Office that all his tax difficulties had been settled and that he was free to leave and to return within six months' time. It was not until he had all the necessary papers signed, and had thoroughly satisfied himself and his attorney that every detail was in order, that Oona had written to me with the news that they would definitely be arriving for the opening. But the political persecution that had begun in the mid-forties with charges of "Communist" activity brought against him by right-wing Congressmen and various veterans' groups, and that had helped to inspire the sordid indictment under the Mann Act of which he had been acquitted in a federal court, was finally to achieve its goal and drive him from the country as an undesirable alien. He did not return to the United States until 1971; a frail and ailing man of eighty-two, he flew to New York with Oona to accept the freedom of the city from Mayor John Lindsay, and then to Hollywood, to receive a special award from the Academy of Motion Pictures.

Naturally there was enormous excitement in England before the Chaplins' arrival at Southampton: what had begun as the famous native son's first triumphant visit to London in twenty years had been transformed into something rather more poignant and terrible.

When I arrived at the Savoy to have tea with Oona, the hotel entrance was crowded with Londoners. I was recognized from my photographs in the press, and several Chaplin well-wishers called out to me, all with more or less the same message to deliver to his suite. "Good old Charlie, tell him we're with him."

I was relieved to find that Chaplin had already gone out to deal with his new difficulties, and wouldn't be back until later that afternoon. I would have been nervous to see him again under any circumstances; given the gravity of the situation, the last thing I wanted was to be in his way. Oona was extraordinarily calm about what had happened, and even tried comforting me by telling me that there had been a prerelease showing of *Limelight* at the Press Academy Theatre in Hollywood and that the film had been warmly received. What the response of the American public would be, now that Chaplin had been banished from the country, was, she admitted, something that nobody could tell. She said that she wasn't sure whether Chaplin would ever want to return to the United States, even if he should be allowed to by a court of appeals or a government decree. She herself was planning to fly back alone to Los Angeles very shortly to close up the house, dismiss the staff who had worked for them since they were first married, and remove from the safe deposit box in the bank all the documents pertaining to the Chaplin studios and the family's financial affairs. In the light of the action already taken without much thought to the niceties of law or honor, Chaplin was fearful that the contents of his safe deposit box might be confiscated by the authorities. Oona dreaded the journey and all that went with closing down a house she'd loved and looked after for eight years, but there was no one to do it but herself and she was ready to leave immediately if that was Charlie's decision. Chaplin arrived back at the hotel a little while later and was far too preoccupied with the injustice done to himself and his family to take much notice of my arrival. He greeted me like someone he hadn't seen for six hours rather than six months, which was just as well with me.

Some days later, when the first shock had worn off, he took me for a walk around Covent Garden. It was then still the largest fruit and vegetable market in the country, a vibrant, colourful district of London that for a long time he had been wanting to see again. Word soon got around among the stallholders that he was there, and quietly they came and stood waiting for him to pass. No one stepped forward to ask for an autograph or even to talk to him. All each man did was put his hand to his forehead in an informal salute, and say, "Hello Guv'nor." It was a display of affection that touched him to the heart. It was a royal progress. I'll never forget it.

Oona left abruptly one day for Los Angeles and I

got on with my play. Then on the Sunday before *Limelight* was to open at the Odeon Theatre, the sign for the film was put up. I took the tube to Leicester Square to see it. I was only mildly surprised to find that Chaplin had given me billing almost equal to his. I hadn't expected anything like it, yet I just accepted it as part of the good fortune streaming my way.

I still hadn't seen the completed *Limelight,* and as I would be performing at the Old Vic on the night of the premiere, I went with Chaplin that morning to see the press screening at the Odeon. Sitting next to him in the front row of the dress circle, waiting for the projectionist to roll the film, I ran through the scenes that we had done together and tried to recall from the rushes I'd seen whether they could have been any good. Then the lights went out and the theme music from *Limelight* began, and very soon I knew why I had been so happy during the months I'd spent on the film: in *Limelight* I had been playing out a girlhood dream inspired by my broken family—the dream of the fairy godfather. Chaplin, with his deep intuition about human types, had been able to focus all that hunger into my performance. The physical resemblance to Oona hadn't been merely skin deep; it was a reflection, rather, of a need we had in common, the need that she herself summed up years later, when she said, "When I was young he took care of me. Now I take care of him." The dream inherent in the story—the dream of the fairy godfather who comes to look after the ailing girl, who heals her with his loving presence, then steps aside for her to assume her glorious role in the world—this dream was rooted so deeply in my real life that even the youthful

crudities of my performance seemed to me overshadowed
by my fervour and conviction in the role. Chaplin's performance struck me as noble, and to flow from that single
poignant word with which he replies to Theresa at the
end of the film, when she tells him in the wings of the
theatre, "I love you." "Really?" he replies, with wry disbe-
lief. The question Chaplin was asking in *Limelight*, for reasons of his own, was, "How can youth love age?" The
answer given by his film was, "Through the magic of
charm." It was the most charming movie I'd ever seen,
and in the last few minutes, with Keaton at the piano
and Chaplin on the violin clowning together in a music
hall skit, one of the funniest. In the hapless destruction
and miraculous resurrection of the musical instruments
there seemed a farcical undoing of all the film's emotional
seriousness about human breakdown and recovery. So,
in the end, that wasn't just funny either—it was heart-
breaking, like everything he conceived.

The film finished, the lights went up, and at first nobody moved. Then they just silently left their seats and
disappeared. From the tension of watching myself on the
screen—in the presence of the London press, no less—I
was exhausted and couldn't speak either. Chaplin seemed
to understand my silence and didn't say anything. Silently
we headed into the foyer, and there, looking down, saw
the people from the press waiting below. When Chaplin
appeared at the top of the staircase with me at his side
they began to applaud and just kept applauding while
we stood there. It was so unexpected—and so marvellous—
that impulsively I turned toward Chaplin and in front
of all those strangers threw my arms around his neck and

kissed him. He had finally made me natural with him in
life as well.

Some three weeks after the opening of *Limelight* Eddie
returned unexpectedly from South Africa, where he had
been living since leaving our family home in Curzon Street
seven years before. He came back alone—his new wife,
Bertha, was to join him later. In South Africa it had seemed
for a while that he was on the way to the affluent life
that had always eluded him. Bertha's family had invested
£5,000—a large sum in 1951—in a new company he had
formed for the production of commercial films for television, and that business had begun with all the promise
of succeeding. However, like almost everything in his life,
the enterprise was mistimed and miscalculated, and he
was once more on the downgrade. He had also had a fairly
severe heart attack some time before he arrived back in
England, although of this I had been told nothing. Whether
he decided to return home for reasons of health or in
the hope of finding yet again a backer who could help
his fortunes, I never knew.

He was sitting in front of the electric fire when I
returned home for my usual rest between the matinee and
evening performances. My mother sat opposite him. Unlike her, he looked completely at home, behaving as though
he had never been away, as though she were still his wife,
and this the familiar hearth. My mother was terribly confused, and didn't know what to make of his return. I wasn't
confused at all. To any display of affection between us,
my resistance was absolute. He had left us to fend for
ourselves and we had done so. I had made a success of

my life so far and was supporting our family in his place. Another actress, Bette Davis, has written of her early life, "I was a self-made man; my father made me one." The statement crystallizes my own attitude on seeing Eddie in our living room that day, and explains the feelings of angry, contemptuous aloofness that I made no effort to disguise.

To make matters worse, he tried giving me advice on my career. I resented the presumption and refused to listen. When he then became somewhat floridly complimentary about my success, I despised that too. I knew even at that moment that I must be being unjust, but nonetheless I wondered if my success wasn't what had brought him back and if I might not be the backer he was looking for in London. My mother was uncomfortable because she knew very well that this was all Eddie's play-acting, and that as soon as Bertha arrived he'd have neither time nor inclination to come around and charm us in the novel role of father and husband. My brother John, by then a young man of seventeen, simply refused to come home for the weekend breaks from Westminster, where he was still a weekly boarder, so long as Eddie was in the vicinity. By 1952, John hardly remembered Eddie and what he remembered he didn't like. Understandably, John was becoming increasingly troubled by the fact that his school fees were largely being paid by his sister, and Eddie's return only dramatised that discomfort.

Happily for all of us Bertha soon arrived in London and the daily paternal visits that I dreaded gave way to an occasional telephone call. But one night during the interval, flowers arrived backstage with a note from Eddie saying that he and Bertha were out front and would like to come round and take me to dinner after the show. I hadn't offered to get tickets for him and was stunned—rather stupidly—to discover that he had arranged to get them himself. During the second half of the play I could barely concentrate on my performance. I kept thinking that if I accepted the invitation to dine with Bertha I would be betraying my mother. I didn't know what to do, and performing in Shakespeare wasn't the easiest place to figure it out. As soon as I returned to my dressing room after the play, the stage door man announced that my father and his wife would like to come up to see me. Instead of asking them into my dressing room for a drink, which I might have done simply out of politeness, I rushed halfway down the corridor to meet them there. Eddie was with an extremely tiny, dark-haired woman who couldn't have looked more inoffensive or been more pleasant. He introduced her as my stepmother, thus opening the way for me to play my scene. Shying away from the poor woman as though I had seen a basilisk, I said that I had no stepmother—my own mother was still living. After an uncomfortable silence, Bertha asked if I would have dinner with them. I refused, they left, and suddenly I felt humiliated on Eddie's behalf, and cruel and shabby on my own. I had handled everything as badly as I possibly could.

Then, a week later, the phone rang, and my mother answered. She started to repeat hysterically, "No! No! No!" I shouted at her, terrified, asking what had happened. "Eddie's dead. He's dead," she said. A friend drove us immediately to the flat Eddie and Bertha had rented near Great

Portland Street, and we went upstairs. Bertha and her sister were sitting in the living room with the curtains drawn. It was still very early in the morning. Bertha, who'd seemed tiny enough when I met her at the theatre, looked smaller still, shrunk into an armchair and unable to speak. Her sister told us that the evening before, Eddie had played a game of bridge with some friends, including my Uncle David, my mother's brother, with whom I didn't even know he was still in touch. When they all left, Eddie said what a wonderful evening it had been. Then he went to bed and died quietly in his sleep, so quietly that Bertha didn't know it until he'd been dead of a thrombosis several hours. He was forty-two years old.

Bertha's sister asked if we would like to see him. She said he looked so peaceful. I was afraid to see a dead person, but having said no to Eddie once too often, I nodded my head and with my mother went into the bedroom. There she touched his face and said goodbye, and I did the same. He lay in his bed on his side, and, except for the waxen colour of his face and the icy feel of his cheek, he did indeed seem at peace, with his head gently resting on his open hand. It is hardly necessary to point out that looking down at him I believed that it was my callous behaviour at the theatre that had killed him.

☆2☆
AFTER

Reflections on Screaming and Dying

⊾ From Juliet to Blanche du Bois

There is no reason to go on telling my story as a story—the story is over, insomuch as it reveals a childhood and an apprenticeship somewhat out of the ordinary. After twenty-two, my private and my professional life began to conform somewhat more to the norm: trial and error, success and failure, obstruction and breakthrough, and then again obstruction.

Since I first achieved recognition as an actress in my early twenties, I have lived more, I have had my share of experience, with the result that I have a little more understanding of the parts I'm playing. What could I know at twenty-two, when I was playing Princess Anne in *Richard III,* about a widow's grief over her husband's murdered body? How could I understand her surrender to the murderer over her husband's coffin? Of course, at the beginning I mostly played parts appropriate to my years—romantic characters, reckless, desperate, mad . . . lyrical like

Ophelia and Juliet, obstinate like Viola, innocent like Miranda.

To be sure, in preparing a role, I always did my homework, read everything I could find about the play and the period and the historical figures. But at the beginning I really didn't know how to go about exploring a script. I generalised instead. "She felt this and she felt that," I'd tell myself, rather than figuring out why specifically she *says* this, why these words at this moment. But I was quick to pick things up, so I thought I understood more than I did. What I understood was superficial. I didn't understand Shakespeare as much as I was carried along—and carried away—by all that sound and emotion. That's what got me through. I relied on the big emotions: love, fear, terror, joy. It worked for me, but it wouldn't now. It worked for anyone who didn't ask too many questions. It terrifies me when I think how recklessly I went plunging into those parts.

Part of my problem was the way Shakespeare was approached when I was a young actress. I doubt if he was "approached" at all. He was *done*. I myself wouldn't have known then how to remedy the faults of those productions, though I was aware of them even at the time. They were superficial, they were "pretty," they were decorative, they were gimmicky, like our beautiful production of *Hamlet* that used a Victorian setting. But to clear away the Victorian rubbish and get to the true relationships between the people—well, I don't remember even one conversation about that. I don't say the actors didn't have them. We did, in our dressing rooms. But I don't remember any director dealing with that, ever. You had to work out by yourself what you were doing and why. I went through a bad period at the Old Vic, after I had been there two years, of trying to work out what I was doing instead of just doing it. The idea was good, but the result was that on stage I lost all spontaneity and everything became deliberate. This came across to the critics as coldness and they let me know it. Cold, frigid, removed, etc. I probably could have got away with it at a provincial rep, but I was doing it at the Old Vic, having become this baby star. I was one of those actresses who had to do her growing up in public: to discover her kind of acting while acting.

No, not my kind of acting. Better to say that there's a style of acting that I admire and that I've tried to develop in my way. This is the performance that's totally in control of uncontrollable emotions, rather than the performance that displays everything, that overwhelms. It may seem at first glance that I'm describing good acting as opposed to bad acting, but I'm not. There are people who can get away with the big, flamboyant effects. It's not a matter of being controlled or uncontrolled—it's a matter of temperament. You have to *have* it. Few women do, actually, but men like Olivier certainly do, and Alan Howard. Vanessa Redgrave, in *Lady from the Sea,* seemed to me to have that bigness. I couldn't begin to have it. I have to work to persuade the audience of my existence, in my role, another way. But that's not something you realise about yourself right off. When I played Blanche du Bois in *A Streetcar Named Desire* in 1974 it may have appeared to people that I had suddenly become a flamboyant, highly theatrical actress. But that was because I was playing a very *withdrawn* woman. I was bold in *Streetcar* because the character was so lyrical and so withdrawn. Not so far from Juliet as you might think.

I come back to Juliet because it was the pivotal performance of my young life. I played it twice. Once when I was twenty-one and then when I was twenty-five, by which time I think I was already too old. I come back to Juliet because it was the first major part I played, the first time I carried a play—a company too, in a way—on my shoulders. And it tasted very good; I liked it. It was being the leading actress rather than playing Ophelia to somebody's Hamlet. Juliet was a perfect role. She starts as a young childish girl and ends up as a tragic woman. Few women's roles allow for that kind of growth. It was a totally satisfying part, complete and great, though it was only about twice a week out of the eight performances that I thought I had fulfilled it. I was accepted as a leading young actress and that gave me the confidence to go forward. Strangely, immediate acceptance carried me straight into self-consciousness and the phase where I began to try to analyse for myself in public what was behind the effect I had made. I had begun to fear that there wasn't much. An enormous early success like mine soon makes you wonder if you haven't got away with murder.

The next pivotal performance was in 1958 in the film *Look Back in Anger*. It was the first time that I felt permission to try things out, and that was largely because of the director, Tony Richardson. I was twenty-seven and playing the part of a young woman of about my own age rather than the young passionate girls I'd portrayed on the stage. I began to feel my own maturity. It was only a beginning, to be sure. The theatrical directors I'd worked with until then had plotted and planned a *production,* whereas Richardson was creating a reality, a thing alive. He would ask, "What would you do here?" or he said, "Go ahead, try it if you want to—let's see what happens." Everybody else I'd worked for seemed to know beforehand what they wanted to happen and so generally nothing but that happened. Richardson gave you freedom. I also helped myself by not going to the rushes. Consequently I wasn't so worried about what I was going to look like as I'd been in my first films. I had no idea of what I was coming across like on the screen—I just knew that what I was doing felt real. It had to do with the world people lived in rather than with the romantic world I pretended to be a part of in my stage performances and that had grown straight out of the fairy tales I'd been brought up on. It helped, too, not to be doing a "classic." That could have its constraining effect twenty-five years ago.

After *Look Back in Anger,* the next pivotal performance was getting married in 1959. One of the great pivotal performances and, for an actress's career, one of the worst. Your career stops. For the next ten years everything I did was a compromise between looking after my child and working. The work came second. The best thing to happen to me as an actress in those years was working with Michael Cacoyannis in *The Trojan Women* at Spoleto in the summer of 1963. There were only two performances, but we rehearsed for three weeks. Cacoyannis did me a tremendous service: he wiped out my appalling sentimentality. I'd seen it in myself on the screen and couldn't bear it. I saw it in my face, I heard it in my voice, but I couldn't

fight it by myself. It had to do with wanting to be loved.
It had to do with *being* loved. I didn't realise that I wanted
that love as much as I did. The result was playing with
sentiment—playing with mine, playing with theirs—rather
than delivering a clean, true emotion. Cacoyannis saw this
and the minute I came out with it, every time, he would
stop me. He even altered my way of speaking verse. No
one should have had to tell me how to speak verse by
that time—it's symptomatic of how little thoughtful direction I had received. Cacoyannis bullied me terribly. I
needed it and I've never forgotten it.

Juliet. Tony Richardson. Getting married. Having a
child. Michael Cacoyannis. The next pivotal experience:
A Doll's House in 1970. It was my part and I'd always known
it, and the only problem was to get somebody to put it
on. I'd been trying to convince producers for years. In
that character were my two halves: the frivolous, silly,
childish woman, and the stern woman. I wouldn't say I
learned anything from playing Nora; rather, I assimilated
all my experience as a woman and brought it together
as an actress. It was a big success, and that was fine, but
I learned nothing new because it came so easily. I don't
remember a moment's difficulty from the first rehearsal
through the run in New York, the film, the run in London.
I don't remember a performance I didn't enjoy. It was
also gratifying because it had been my idea to do it. I
was involved in the production, I helped to cast it, I chose
the director, even the designer. That had never happened
to me before. When I had tried over the years to get people
to produce *A Doll's House* they all told me, "Oh, no, it's
an old-fashioned play, it's no good," and yet I *knew* that
it was a wonderful play and also a timely play—that it

was about practically every woman I'd known who wanted something more from her life. And so that first performance, when the audience applauded and then came down in a great state of excitement and stood in front of the stage, I realised I'd been right. It wasn't just the pleasure of playing another childish creature who ends up as a woman—because Nora too is in a line of sorts from Juliet; it was that I was justified in my faith, and also, I must say, justified in making people put up a lot of money for this idea of mine. And it went on from there. The play was taken up by the women's movement—and by women, apart from any movement—and the theatre was full each night with a tremendously receptive audience. We could have run much longer than the six months. We went on tour for eight weeks, then the film, then the London stage for six months. And I never tired of it. There was some contact between the audience and us that I'd never experienced before. I thought, "This must be what a politician feels," when I would hear their response to lines in the last scene. You were speaking to people's longings. It's rare to be moved by the audience—that's getting things back to front—but that happened.

The pivotal performance that came next was in '74 in *A Streetcar Named Desire*. Apart from Hedda Gabler, Blanche du Bois may be the best role for a woman that exists in modern drama. For me, doing it helped to break down my image as a porcelain figure. Even after *A Doll's House*, those clichés about "the English rose" came back at me and nearly drove me mad. Actually, Blanche du Bois is extremely near my own—I suppose "breaking-point" is the word. There's a side of me that isn't very well balanced, that's nervous and neurotic and will go from one disaster to the next. That was all there in the role. And I didn't have to look far to verify her behaviour. People *thought* that it was a tremendous breakthrough and that I was playing a whore, which of course she isn't. People have crude expectations and there's no way around it. But I got the *Evening Standard* Award for the Best Actress of the Year. I got the Variety Club Best Actress Award and I got the Plays and Players Award. I got things that I wanted.

Ed Sherin directed *Streetcar* without directing. He was deft in the way Tony Richardson had been—he just guided you gently into your own performance. He was outside it and let you do it, but paid attention all the while. The next time I worked with Sherin—in a Tennessee Williams play that never reached Broadway—he was anything but deft. He made the actors' life hell. But that play wasn't *Streetcar*, and he didn't know what to do with it, and the result was artistic confusion and bitterness all around. However, with *Streetcar* I had my freedom again—the freedom of not having to please, the freedom to invent without satisfying the director, or one's mother, or the audience. I had been trying to learn that all along. It was hard for me because I had tried to please my mother for so long, and then I had tried to please my Aunt Mary. It's only in the last ten years that I haven't thought whether Mary would have approved of the way I was doing a line. I don't mean to suggest that Mary had a limited idea of acting inside of which I felt trapped. She had broad intelligence and tremendous critical faculties. There were worse people to try to please. As for my mother, though it was always hard for me to accept criticism from her, I never knew her sense of my performance to be wrong. I don't mean I was limited by trying to please people who were themselves limited—I was limited by trying to please.

I try to recall if there are other actors who have influenced my own acting as much as directors like Richardson and Cacoyannis, and the answer is no. I don't know how you learn from watching other actors. My Aunt Mary was an enormous influence, but that was through her wit and intelligence and taste, not by her acting. In Irene Worth, a lifelong friend, I also discovered someone who was a marvellous actress and a remarkable woman. We met at the Old Vic in *The Merchant of Venice.* I was a dreadful Jessica, and though her Portia was better, it wasn't the great performance of a career. It was her seriousness that I admired so, her sense of her work as a life-and-death challenge. I was vastly relieved by meeting someone with Irene's depth—I had always been afraid that acting produced a hollowness in people. That was a bit stupid, because I already knew Sybil Thorndike, I knew some remarkable people—so I suppose I was afraid that the hollow person acting might produce would be me.

I was twenty-seven years old when I met Vivien Leigh. We played together in 1958 in *Duel of Angels.* When you're still in your twenties and come into the sphere of such a woman, you are *influenced.* On the stage she wasn't the world's most wonderful actress, but altogether she was most astonishing. By now there's a myth about her magic, but she had just that. Over other women, and certainly over men, she cast an extraordinary spell. I don't know that I ever heard her say anything profound or knew her to read anything demanding. I also thought she was a social snob, though I now realise that she was simply interested in interesting people and they were people generally who were well known. Of course her beauty was inconceivable. She really was the most beautiful woman in the world. We acted together, but she influenced me much more in the way I wanted to present myself—to dress, to be, my manner, the way to run a house, the way to enjoy the world—influenced me much more as a woman than as an actress. She showed me how an actress *could* be a woman, as John Gielgud, the most splendid of actors, showed me how an actor could be a gentleman. It sounds strange, finding in Vivien Leigh a model of how to join your profession to your whole life, because her own life was finally so tragic. She was breakable, that was very much a part of her—that terror and anxiety and delicacy and fear. But she was also so precise and clean and ordered. I think she was the first orderly person I ever met. Everything had to be in its place and everything had to be perfect. That orderliness was in her work too. In *Duel of Angels* she gave the same performance on the last night as she did at the first rehearsal. It was all worked out and so without real spontaneity. But she had spontaneity as a woman—she had everything. She was extraordinary.

ⱪ Banging My Head Against the Wall, and Other Secrets of the Craft

Actors are asked how they manage to keep a stage performance spontaneous when, to some degree certainly, it *has* been worked out in every detail beforehand, and

then repeated over again night after night. I myself have
tried all sorts of things. Before I went onstage when I
was young, I used to try to relax by saying the Hail Mary
three times. It was something to drag me away from the
daytime self and the jittery nerves. During the tour of
A Doll's House, when we were in Toronto, I went to somebody high up in the meditation business and he gave me
a mantra. The same sort of thing. Generally before a performance I'm either trying to calm myself down or trying
to work myself up. The method I devised for working
myself up I first learned while doing films, where insta-
matic acting is required and you have to find yourself
emotionally in the middle of a scene, having done the
beginning of it the Christmas before last. I would run
what I call "tapes" in my mind—tapes of events in my
life that had been deeply affecting. They had to be dreadful
in order to have the desired effect: appalling disasters, terrible humiliations, wrenching losses, etc. They were what
worked me up into a heightened emotional state. I would
try to get myself to the brink of tears and then control
them and start the scene from there. I used this technique
in *A Streetcar Named Desire* and *Hedda Gabler,* where my parts
were full of tension from the first word that's spoken.
In *A Doll's House* I didn't have to, because Nora enters so
happy. When I was very young, seventeen, I used to bang
my head against the wall before Ophelia's mad scene. It's
the same principle. At seventeen I had no appropriate
memories for that role, no tapes to play, and so I used
to stand in front of a radiator—I still remember the warmth
on my back—and bang my head against the wall in my
dressing room at Stratford-upon-Avon. No tapes, and no

technique to speak of either, and I didn't know how else to find the emotion. Ophelia, after all, is not a weighty part. It's really rather light: there are only four scenes, and they're widely spaced through the play—the mad scene doesn't occur until some forty minutes after the play-within-the-play scene, which is the last time Ophelia's been seen. Somehow or other, you do have to work yourself up again each time. Fortunately for me, in repertory, we played *Hamlet* only twice a week.

Simply, the point is that if you wheel around like a dervish or say your mantra or repeat Hail Mary three times—whatever incantation you intone on this night or that—you are attempting to put yourself into a state where you are receptive, where you can take in and then give out. Once, during the rehearsals for *Streetcar*, when Ed Sherin saw me working myself up with this carry-on of mine, he was horrified. He said, "What actually are you doing?" He was the first person I ever told about the secret tapes, and he thought they were a bad idea. He said, for one thing you can only play a tape so many times—and what happens if you can't get the machine to go at all? I said that was true, I was always worried that the tapes might not play when I needed them. "Then empty yourself," he said, "completely empty yourself of everything, and breathe, and make your mind as much of a blank as you can." Which, of course, is the function of the mantra, too. "When you come on," he said, "slowly fill yourself with what is happening *on* the stage, rather than bringing with you a prefabricated excitement that has nothing to do with the play and has to be superimposed upon it." Good advice—I tried that too. I'll try anything. In the silent film era, the stars used to have a violinist on the set, to get them going. The Actors Studio devised a whole vocabulary about the relationship between the actor and his role, and about the character's motivation. But often their language struck my ear as jargon and seemed to me to put plain things pretentiously.

Perhaps it was useless to me because I come from a very different tradition of acting and don't really know what the "Method" is. I've been told that Method acting is an enormous exposure of what you are—accent on enormous and you. Yet, when one meets in the flesh the you who's been exposing himself enormously, one often finds that there's no one there, no self at all. No, the Method lingo has never explained to me the mystery of a performance, particularly a good one. I always have thought that, in fact, the Method had more to do with a certain social class being permitted to bring its style of response onto the stage and the screen than with the psychology of acting. At times Method theory could not help but confuse the expressiveness of American immigrant society and the American working class with human behaviour generally. Witness Brando in *Julius Caesar*. Unquestionably the brilliant Method performances I've seen have been in working-class roles, like Brando's in *On the Waterfront*. Finally, all acting technique aims for the same result: to get you into a psychological position where you can release your intuitive knowledge of life, however large or small. Any technique that doesn't do that for you comes out as mannerism.

The only actor I knew at all well who'd had Method training was my first husband, Rod Steiger. I did learn

something valuable from him, but it wasn't the secret to
the Method—it was plain boldness. This had more to do
with his temperament than with his training. I once saw
him do something extraordinary when we were making
the film *Three Into Two Won't Go*. We played a husband
and wife in trouble. He had a scene at the end where he
had to come into the house drunk. Sitting watching him
were me as his wife and Peggy Ashcroft as his mother-
in-law—a difficult silent audience. He came in and played
the scene in the most appalling way. The English contin-
gent, Peggy and I and the director Peter Hall, were dumb-
struck. He'd been all over the place, no control, no sense,
just the spewing out of a scene. Peter Hall said to me,
"Can you speak to him?" I said, "I have nothing to do
with him as an actor. I'm here to play my part and he's
here to play his part, and I wouldn't dream of it." And
he said, "But what about *that?*" I said, "Well, I've never
seen anything so terrible in my life." So we took it again
and he controlled it somewhat, and then we did a third
take, and on the fourth he was wonderful. It taught me,
as I said, a certain boldness. Because of my personality,
I start out the opposite way—sizing up a role, I start out
with this small effect and that small effect, and then gradually I begin to breathe and expand and fill it in, and I
end up more or less where everybody else is. I'm sure
that's been difficult for people who've worked with me,
not to mention for producers coming to rehearsals. Watching Steiger I realised that you could as well start from
the top and work your way down, as start from the most
minimal twitchings and stirrings and keep grafting onto
it. Partly what it boils down to is that you can make just

as big a fool of yourself one way as the other.

How else does an actor make a fool of himself? With his failings. In my case, the sentimentality that I've mentioned, appealing for understanding or love, showing too openly an emotion that would be more interesting if it had some opacity, some veneer. I also have to be careful about a certain stridency in my voice, something ugly and grating, when I'm trying to be "strong." Usually the failings take over at moments where one isn't sure of oneself. You cover up with something, and those used to be my two favourites. This can happen in an entire role, of course, if you make the mistake of taking one that isn't for you. In 1978, in my second play with Ed Sherin directing—Tennessee Williams' *Red Devil Battery Sign*—I was nothing but one long shout. I had taken the role because I admired Tennessee Williams and had been so successful in *Streetcar* that I hoped for something to equal it. I should have studied the script with infinitely more care rather than being carried away with the desire to recapitulate my previous experience in a Williams play. However disappointing it was, I should have realised that the role wasn't for me and turned it down. As has been proved since by actors other than me, both the role and the script were quite unplayable, but none of us knew this at the time, and it was a nightmare from beginning to end. When I turned up at the first rehearsal I was told to my amazement that I would have to play the part as a Texan. Sherin and the producer had decided this only the day before. Well, I'd never even been to Texas. I didn't even know a Texan. I didn't know what I was doing, so I started to shout.

Every actor has his way of signalling that he's in over his head and doesn't know how to get out. It's a professional affliction that almost no one escapes: suddenly this splendid actor begins to emote profusely, and if you know him, you know something's wrong. This one turns to camp, that one looks in the air, this one waves his hands about, that one clenches her fists and then violently overacts. I have a little gesture that's an obvious sign of tension— the arm is straight down and I raise my wrist so my hand is parallel to the ground. It's a physical sign of my uncertainty, and I know it the instant I do it. It's like something you might do out of nervousness at a cocktail party. You put on some kind of face or voice, some act that you know isn't yourself but that you hope will get you by until you can get the hell out of there and on to something else.

Fortunately, it isn't often that I've wound up in roles for which I was ill-suited. There was *Red Devil Battery Sign*, and back in 1963, there was Sartre's *The Condemned of Altona*. I thought I was to be a German intellectual actress, a kind of Brechtian actress like a young Helene Weigel, but the director kept telling me that she was a star like Marilyn Monroe. In rehearsal I said, "You know, you must get someone else to play this, because if this is the way you see it, then I can't do it at all." Fortunately we had a break and I took myself off to Amsterdam for the weekend. I just thought, to hell with it. When I got back to London I rang him and said, "Where do we go from here? What are we going to do?" He said, "Well, let's try it your way and see if we can come together somehow in the end." But the result was that I no longer had a clear view of who this woman was, and so I couldn't get her either way. I realised too late that I'd chosen the wrong role. The interesting part was the incestuous sister, and I was angry with myself that I hadn't been clever enough to see that though it was a smaller part it was much better. But a few years earlier my Aunt Mary had seen *The Condemned of Altona* in Paris with Serge Reggiani and had come back and told me that Johanna was a perfect role for me. So when it was offered I thought, "Oh, terrific," and mistakenly said yes.

Probably the role that's disappointed me most in my career, and yet one that I thought myself eminently suited for—and, stubbornly, still do—is Rebecca West in Ibsen's *Rosmersholm*. The play was performed in the West End in 1977. It was a part I had longed to play and yet it feels now as though I never did it. There were perhaps two performances—one, strangely enough, on the opening night—when I thought that I came *near* this extraordinary woman: her cunning, her desire, her inwardness and determination. But the atmosphere at rehearsals had been appalling—animosity from the start between the director and me, and then a leading man who was endlessly discussing himself. And the only way to act in *Rosmersholm* is to have a Rosmer who acts with you. There were moments in which I felt a complete amateur, passages I couldn't cope with at all. When I was let free on my own—as in the last act, which is really hers—I was at home. But *Rosmersholm* was a non-event. It didn't happen. It was a mistake ever to try it in the commercial theatre. Not that the audiences were always bad—sometimes they were very good—but it was still an uphill battle, hoping that people would be there and see the damn thing and understand it. It's not so easy for a modern audience to grasp the emotional, moral, and social undercurrents in *Rosmersholm* as it is for them in *A Doll's House.* The odds were against it all the way, and I knew when I went into it that it wasn't at all what I wanted. With John Neville or Paul Scofield as Rosmer, with a production not in the West End . . . but that wasn't the way it was.

To my good fortune, there has been only a handful of these experiences. If the part or the production isn't for me, I can usually tell from reading the script, or talking to the director. That doesn't mean that I won't attempt something not altogether my style if it's on television or film. But not on the stage, where, to my mind, it still counts the most. That's where I started, that's where the work that I wanted to do was being done. Again I come back to the influence of my Aunt Mary, and my early infatuation with Shakespeare. I also know that there's no actress in England of any importance who hasn't made her name on the stage, whose career doesn't continue on the stage, even if she does film or television. When television and films come along, I do them to keep working and to make money. I can't earn a living in the theatre— nobody can. Television or films take a few weeks or a couple of months, whereas a play, by the time you're finished, can take up to eight months and that's even if it doesn't run; by the time you've waited for it, rehearsed it, gone on tour and had a decent run, you can be tied up for over a year. That's another reason to be certain that there's something in it for *you.* In a film, if people are foolish enough to ask you to play something a little bizarre and if the film itself isn't appalling, it's worth the risk. I wouldn't play Lady Bird Johnson when I was asked recently to do her for TV because I would have made a fool of myself. On the other hand, I knew I was wrong casting for the sexpot in *The Chapman Report,* but if as good a director as George Cukor wanted to take a chance, I went ahead with it. Also there's the chance that the director in a film can pull you through—he can't on the stage. In the film the director can direct you moment by moment and then edit you into Duse in the cutting room. The stage isn't the same. You build the role differently. Your contact with the other actors is more intense. In the theatre there are days when it goes badly and days when it's perfect, and so the drama of the whole situation is heightened. I know that ninety million people watch television and nine hundred see a play, but what difference does that make? It's you who's doing what you're doing.

⋉ Actors

Who are they? What are they? Well, all kinds of people become actors—as many kinds as become businessmen—and there are all kinds of actors. There are actors in musicals and actors at the Royal Shakespeare Company. There are actors who are exhibitionists and actors who are painfully shy—for the painfully shy who are actors, acting may be the only painless thing they do. There are

actors who are egomaniacs and actors with practically no
discernible ego. There are actors who are simple and open,
people whose complexity you only really see on the stage,
and there are actors who have so many sides that it's only
on the stage that they can put themselves together and
feel some unified sense of being for a few hours each
night. There are intelligent, reflective actors, and actors,
I suppose, who are stupid, but I don't think you can be
stupid and a good actor. I've never known a stupid good
actor. You have to be alert and that rules out stupidity.
You have to be watching and taking things in. I don't
mean that you study people for your art. You study them
because you're interested in them, the way they talk, the
way they look and move. You have to watch and then
you have to store it away somewhere, in some drawer
marked Miscellaneous.

Lillian Ross wrote what I remember as a good book
called *Actor,* a collection of interviews. I was one of those
interviewed, and a common theme in the book seemed
to be a shared feeling that only on the stage were we
wholly alive and wholly at ease with ourselves. Now
maybe that's what everyone would say about himself in
his work. I walk on the stage and I think, "Oh yes, this
is it," and probably that's what a well-trained machinist
feels when he sits down in front of his tools. That's what
he does best and so that's where he's at home. A mystique
has grown up about acting because it's done in public,
and it isn't done from nine to five, and a character emerges
on a stage who, to the public, is you and yet not you.
But to a skilful and devoted actor, it's the place where
he does his job and finds the satisfactions that come with

doing well the work that one likes. On the other hand, it may be that the machinist doesn't feel quite so unsure of himself outside of his job as so many actors do. I think this emerged from the Lillian Ross book too: people who were rather unsure of themselves as themselves were very sure of themselves when they were being someone else.

Different things drive different people onto the stage. There are obviously those who want to entertain. I must say that thought has never crossed my mind. There are some critics who would contend that maybe it should have. Certainly you feel guilty if you give a bad performance—there is a responsibility to the audience that has paid to come to see you, but the word "entertain" doesn't describe to me what you're responsible for. Still, there are extroverts who have a terrifically good time bringing the house down. I want something wonderful to happen on the stage among the actors. I want to forget the audience, rather the way they, ideally, will forget themselves if all is going well.

The kind of actors I've felt closest to are those who've sought in acting a way of participating in literature. I'm not a creative artist: I don't write, compose, or paint—I interpret what is already written, as a musician interprets Schubert or Brahms. You open a volume of Shakespeare and all you see is a page of print. The actor brings life to that print. The playwright solves the problems of composition, the actor the problems of presentation. Contrary to vulgar opinion, the power an actor feels has nothing to do with exhibiting himself on a stage, but with being able to solve these problems. As for self-exhibition, the point is that it isn't yourself that you're exhibiting. *You* disappear. Far from dominating by the force of ego, you hold sway, if you do, by egolessness. Your ego has to be present in everyday existence in order to fight through life's obstacles. But on the stage there is no interference from the outside. There's only the story, whose outcome you know and whose progression you know, syllable by syllable, from beginning to end; the acting task is to make the story happen again and again, to transform acting into action, language into being. There are limits to the number of times you can convincingly tell the same story, but that you can tell it as often as you do must mean that there's something satisfying to the actor in repeating and repeating his role. As Nora, I used to run on stage in *A Doll's House* with my arms full of packages and see my Christmas tree, and every night I had the same cleansing feeling of relief. I thought, everything else is outside, the complications are at home. I know this story, it's going to unfold like this, I have it in my power to *make* it unfold like this. It was Ibsen who'd imagined the story, but it was for me to demonstrate what he'd imagined.

Of course, one isn't doing Ibsen or Shakespeare or Chekhov every day. There are only so many masterpieces. What gets serious actors through the ordinary stuff that almost everyone has to do just to make a living is something more personal than the idealistic desire to participate in great literature: that is, a limitless capacity to pretend. What makes this capacity limitless I can't say, but certainly what's spoken of, often disparagingly, as the childish and immature side of an actor is his openness to games of disguise and make-believe, a love of self-transformation. What distinguishes this from mere childishness is that the desire to pretend doesn't mean that you know how to pretend. The kind of people who become actors are also people who have developed an actor's skills. In that way they're like the kind of people who become surgeons—a natural talent, genetically bestowed, is nurtured by study and hard work.

I've worked best with actors and I've worked worst with superstars, real or incipient or thwarted. I can't imagine how it could be otherwise for anyone. I've worked best with Donald Madden and Colin Blakely and Timothy West and Martin Shaw and Joss Ackland and Alan Badel and Paul Scofield and Robert Helpmann and Emrys James—actors who are there because they want to play a part and not because they want the part as a vehicle for their ego. Vivien Leigh was lovely to act with; so was Eileen Atkins, so was Irene Worth, and there are many more. It's simple to act with people who will allow themselves to be taken into the play rather than superimposing themselves onto the play. They make it impossible for you to break through to them, and they make it so deliberately. They do it deliberately enough in life; that's what they're out to do. They're like that in life and they're like that on the stage. They're not out to support you, to react to you, to receive from you, to be helped by you— all those lovely things that happen between actors. When you say an actors' company, it is indeed a company, not a place for exhibiting yourself or indulging your power mania. If you want that, then you should go out and sing like Frank Sinatra, or work by yourself somewhere. Perhaps the most astonishing thing in my acting career happened after a rehearsal of *A Doll's House* in New York. One of the actors playing an important part came up to me and said, "Thank you for the eye contact." I thought I had gone mad. But according to him, leading actors acting away by themselves weren't that hard to find in New York. Steiger used to put it very simply: "Acting isn't acting, it's interacting."

Only recently I played Madame Ranyevskaya in *The Cherry Orchard* with Joss Ackland and Emrys James, two actors who gave me everything I could want from fellow performers. Their inspired portrayals of Gayev—Madame Ranyevskaya's childish, charming, ineffectual older brother—and of the merchant Lopakhin—the old family friend who buys up their estate in order to tear it down for country cottages—strongly shaped my own understanding of Madame Ranyevskaya's character, her place in their world of feeling and in their social world, and helped me find the physical bearing that Chekhov considered essential to the role.

What I had to begin with, aside of course from the great play itself, were a few lines that Chekhov had written about Madame Ranyevskaya, in letters to Stanislavsky and others, about the time the play was first performed by the Moscow Art Theatre in 1904. "Not smartly dressed but with great taste. Intelligent, very warm-hearted, inattentive; she is very loving towards everybody, always a smile on her face. . . . No, I never wanted to make Lyuba lose her zest for life. The only thing that would make a woman like her lose that would be death. . . . It is not difficult to play the part of Lyuba provided you get the right tone from the very beginning; one has to find the right kind of smile and manner of laughing, and one must know how to dress."

On a stage you cannot be loving on your own, and what Joss Ackland's Gayev gave me was someone to love: not only a brother in whose blood relationship I could believe, but a brother to protect and indulge, a brother to stroke and kiss and cuddle, a brother whose face his sister would have to clean with her handkerchief after he had overeaten at his "disgusting" restaurant, and whose dishevelled clothes she would have to straighten after his final collapse in Act Four. He gave me a childhood playmate, a companion in nostalgia, above all a needy, naked soul to whom I could extend Ranyevskaya's warm-heartedness. In his fecklessness about their debts and helpless irresponsibility about the fate of their estate, he furnished the comical counterpart to Ranyevskaya's inattentiveness, a deep inattentiveness to consequences no less than conversation, a deep and unforgivable inattentiveness that amounts finally to moral shallowness, and leads to the loss of the cherry orchard that, to me, seemed the original source of her zest for life.

If Joss Ackland's Gayev was the vessel into which I could pour Lyuba's kind of lovingness, in Emrys James' Lopakhin I found the object for her smile. No, it is not difficult to play the part of Lyuba, to find the right kind of smile and manner of laughing, if you have opposite you a Lopakhin of sly but unmistakable sexual charm and aggressive, manly vitality. To be a loving sister on the stage you need a brother who needs your love; to be flirtatious, entertaining, and seductive, you need a man worth the effort. And Emrys James' Lopakhin was such a man. Numerous times early on in rehearsals, Emrys's strong clear response to something still half-realised in my own conception of Ranyevskaya clarified for me the direction to take. I remember one moment during the first week we were rehearsing Act One, when, as Lopakhin, Emrys leaned far over the sofa where I was sitting with my coffee cup in order to tell me that he loved me "like his own flesh and blood." But it was clear from his tone and his gaze and his posture that it wasn't merely like his own flesh and blood that he loved me. The next time we went through the scene, instead of sitting on the sofa to take my coffee, I stretched across the sofa like an odalisque. Let him see a true slave of love! "She's an immoral woman," Gayev says of his sister behind her back, "it's in every movement she makes." Stretched across the sofa under Lopakhin's feasting eyes I felt for the first time something like the woman about whom that observation might be made, even a little unjustly.

I remember another moment, again during an early rehearsal of Act One, when in response to Lopakhin's initial suggestion that the cherry orchard be chopped down to make way for lucrative country cottages, I burst into laughter at the absurdity of the idea. Suddenly Emrys began to laugh too—at my laughter. So I laughed even more—and he laughed at that. Then Joss, as Gayev, began to laugh at the two of us laughing. Suddenly a source of worry and concern had been dissipated in the most silly and charming way; suddenly we hadn't to think about paying our debts or selling our estate or chopping down our beloved cherry orchard—we could all have a good time instead. If I laughed enough and enchanted him enough, all the bad things would magically just disappear.

Yes, I thought, this was the form that her inattentiveness would take. Needless to say, it would have been quite impossible to register inattention had there not been beside me a Lopakhin so capable of commanding attention.

I've acted with John Gielgud, Laurence Olivier, and Ralph Richardson, and I should like to say something here about their special qualities. To begin with Gielgud, there is his personal beauty. He was the most beautiful man. I'll never forget seeing him in *Hamlet* in 1946—the picture of him, sitting in his chair: he had a white square collar insert and the black tunic and this long, long neck, and wonderful elevated head and piercing blue eyes—eyes piercing with intelligence. Then there was his voice, the most lyrical voice that's ever been heard on the English stage. Lyrical, yet guided always by intelligence. Then there's that tremendous nervous tension you feel with him all the time. And so delicate: subtle, sensitive, and open to everything around him. And, of course, tasteful to a degree. I think he's the greatest Hamlet we'll ever see, I should think the greatest Hamlet that's ever been.

With Olivier there was sex and excitement, the masculine drive, the electric vibrancy—even his voice was like electricity, high, sharp, and staccato. He had tremendous personal glamour. Obviously you can't be a great actor without having that. Though, strangely, Richardson doesn't. He has genius of an eccentric kind. Richardson could be more moving than anybody—his Vanya, his Peer Gynt. He isn't guarded in any way. That's how he moves you so. That's why, as a man, he says all these strange and peculiar things—because the censor isn't there. And of course he's extremely intelligent. Great warmth, great vitality, great intelligence.

The one I've acted with most is Gielgud. In *The Lady's Not for Burning* he was both director and star—a man in his mid-forties, and I was just eighteen. Then in *Lear*, I was his Cordelia. I had taken over the role from Peggy Ashcroft, in a peculiar production of George Devine's with Japanese costumes and sets. Then we did Chekhov's *Ivanov* together; I played Sasha opposite his Ivanov. In each play working with him was quite different. As a young girl I was simply terrified of him, that's all. It was as Cordelia, particularly in what's called the recognition scene—when he's brought on in a coma—that I realised how *easy* it was to act opposite him. But it was a difficult production, and half the time was spent pushing him back on his bed, a piece of modeled sculpture by Noguchi. Everything was a piece of modeled sculpture by Noguchi. The sculpture that was the bed was slanted at an angle, and so he had one hell of a time just being in the coma. There were so many things to worry about, I was never completely free to enjoy him. But when we did *Ivanov*, I think we acted very well together. In the last scene, when Sasha has forced him, really, to marry her . . . he doesn't want to, he's twenty years older than she is and he's terrified; he feels himself a complete failure, and she, with the terrifying drive of youth, *makes* him marry her, tells him that together they can be this-that-and-the-other . . . well, he entered in that last scene dressed as a bridegroom, and I was in my wedding dress, and there was something about

him, the minute I saw him, that made me start to cry.
He came on in such a state you could *only* cry. John Gielgud
cries very easily, but I don't. But when he said, "Oh, my
God, look at me, I'm an old man and there's grey in my
hair, and I can't go through with it," I didn't have to do
what is called "acting." We reached an emotional pitch
together in that scene that I had never felt with anybody
else.

The Audience

There actually are such things as a bad audience and
a good audience. You can tell from the moment the curtain
goes up if they're extreme in either way. It doesn't mean
that a bad audience can't end up as a good audience, and
you can certainly lose a good audience and it can end
up a bad audience. They feel you so immediately when
they're good, and if you're not one hundred percent alert
or alive, they get discouraged. Then you can get a dud
audience that for some reason, en masse, has no idea what
you're doing. They just sit there. They don't react in any
way. They just give off this low, steady, rustling sound
that says, "We're not here." The dud audience seems to
me to turn up with most regularity on Thursday nights.
The only reason I can think of is that the television in
England used to be so good on Thursday that most sensible
people were at home watching. Then on Saturday night

you'll get people who drop in because there's nothing else
to do, but sometimes they can be exciting, those pleasure-
seekers.

What you get from a good audience is silence—not
the silence of sleep or lethargy, but the silence of concen-
tration. You can tell the difference. I had a long speech
in *Rosmersholm*—one of the few in that play that had been
right from the beginning—and there was a long pause I
held in the middle of it, and I knew from the quality of
the silence that I could hold it and hold it and they'd be
with me. Obviously you feel the presence of the good
audience most directly in comedy. The laughs are quick
and easy. Unfortunately I've done little comedy, but in
the first act of *A Doll's House* there were a lot of laughs—
many of them laughs that we found, to lighten the beginning. It was a delicious feeling just to *play* with people—
to know they are with you, and following you, and appre-
ciating what you do.

Obviously it's depressing if the house is empty, especially if the whole thing is going downhill. But if it's not,
and it's just an empty house, that doesn't mean the end
of the world; you can give a strangely good performance
under those circumstances, at a matinee particularly. *Streetcar* was performed in a big theatre that was jammed every
night but was empty at matinees. Who wants to go and
see that play at the matinee? I used to look out at that
huge auditorium, and there was the long center aisle, and
all the way down two people on either side. It's like looking
down the map of Egypt and there's the Nile and nothing
else. I was in despair, but sometimes, because I was also

so relaxed, marvellous things would happen.

The closest I've come to an ideal audience was off Broadway. Certainly never on Broadway. On Broadway I would say I played almost consistently to dud audiences. Off Broadway was completely different. We were doing *A Doll's House* and *Hedda Gabler*, and people came because they wanted to see Ibsen. The seats were far cheaper than on Broadway, young people could afford them, and the theatre seated five hundred as opposed to a thousand or twelve hundred. These were people who'd come not just to be entertained, but to listen and to be drawn in.

It's hard for me to say what the difference is between playing for an American and an English theatre audience. I come to America as a foreigner, generally doing a play that's a little exotic to an American audience. In New York in 1972 Eileen Atkins and I did *Vivat! Vivat Regina!*, a play about Elizabeth I and Mary Stuart. The curtain went up, and really, it couldn't have been our fault, because we hadn't even started, and there were two or three people asleep in the first row. They'd had their dinner, they'd paid their money, and they were out. Mainly men—they came hating the play and hating the women who'd dragged them to it. There was a scene in *Vivat* where I used to bang the table to make a point to Bothwell, and I used to bang it as loud as I could because I wanted to see somebody wake up. But it wasn't their fault they were sleeping. It was a play about England with a title they couldn't understand and two dead women who didn't mean anything to them. Obviously one would have got a much more attentive audience in England. I can't speak with any authority, as an actress, about the American audience. But I find them, when I'm a member of the audience myself, to be very easily pleased. Often when I'm not.

As a result of being in America during my formative years, I've never felt a complete stranger there, in or out of the theatre. I don't feel that I'm part of America, but I feel it's somewhere that I've known all my life. Much that happened to me there as a child was painful, but some of it was quite wonderful; perhaps being there made me more uncertain than I might have been, but it also made me more independent. In the end it left me with the knowledge that one could get out: I had lived somewhere else and I had survived it, and so I knew from then on that there was always some other place to go. There was a price to pay for this knowledge: I felt guilty and embarrassed that I had left England during the war, and for years afterward I always made it clear to whoever asked that I had come back in 1943, just in time for the Little Blitz. Of course our evacuation was in no way up to me—I was nine when it happened, but as most people didn't leave and we did, I felt a little like a traitor. Maybe this accounts for why, late in 1943, when our boat sailed out of Philadelphia harbour for Europe, I spat over the back and swore I'd never return. I was preparing myself for patriotic reentry. I was also of a very dramatic turn of mind.

When I returned to America as an actress in my midtwenties, I liked particularly the feeling of being as yet uncategorized in America. I was by then well known in England and liked escaping to where the audience had as yet no hardened simplification of me. I felt that everything in America was accessible to me, and that in England, young as I was, everything was now ordained, set, decided. I thought that America was an open society and that anything could happen to me there. I could be something other than an English rose—also something other than a daughter, or a granddaughter, or a respectable middle-class girl. Many English actors have had this sense of new, liberating possibilities for themselves on arriving in America. New York represents excitement and glamour, and Hollywood represents—Hollywood. The movies, money. Going to Hollywood after the London stage is a kind of lark. Even to be in a Cecil B. De Mille extravaganza, a film of the sort one had seen and loved as a kid, could be a thrill. It was all on such a big scale. In England it was all much smaller and more serious. *I* was smaller and more serious. In America I found myself dressing less conventionally and even becoming a bit more gregarious. Everyone seemed more direct, and everything seemed so easy, and I liked the comfort of it: good heating and plumbing, stores open till all hours, luncheonettes, and much more money. I escaped the feeling that either I must be doing a great play or I was worthless. My sense of duty, to myself, to everybody, took a holiday. I married an American and lived with him in Manhattan, in Brooklyn Heights, and later in Malibu. I live with an American now, and when I'm not at work in London, I spend some part of the year with him in the New England countryside. However much I "belong" there, I often feel homesick and always feel passionately English, more passionately English in America than when I'm in England. But this may be the evacuee's inheritance, to be drawn in two directions because of being formed as a child in two places.

⟨ *The Life*

When you work in the theatre, you have no day at all—your performance hangs over you all day long. If it's a comedy or a light role, it's not so bad, but if it's a taxing or difficult role and you're doing it eight times a week, you've got to be careful. If you manage to crawl out on your hands and knees and have lunch and have a little walk, that's fine. If you meet someone, or if you want to go to a shop or a museum, well, that's difficult, because you must be resting by four and up again at five to get to the theatre by six-thirty, assuming the performance is at eight. And when it's over, you can't go straight to bed. It's the only time of the day you're hungry, and you want to eat and to drink and talk to your friends and have a good time; if you don't have that then, you don't have it at all. So you don't get to bed until one or two, and ideally, you shouldn't wake up until eleven. In London, when the day is short and it's dark at four and you don't get out of the house till twelve-thirty or one, it's like living in the city of dreadful night. On a matinee day you get up, you have a very light lunch, you go to the theatre, you do the performance, you have an avocado, you go to sleep and then you wake up—you try to wake up—to do the next performance. If you're playing in repertory and have a couple of nights off, then you have a way of stoking yourself up again. But in the commercial theatre, if you have two performances on Saturday, they leave you totally exhausted on Sunday. And by Monday morning, when you're beginning to feel better, it starts again.

At the beginning, the acting is sufficient compensation for the inroads that this makes into a regular pattern of living. But eventually, in my case, I wanted a family as well as my career. I wanted to have children. I wanted to be married—I couldn't imagine my life unmarried. I was determined to try to have both, the marriage with children *and* the career, but it didn't work.

It was the marriage that didn't work, for a start. I've noticed this with actresses: either you have a man as a servant who will come with you when you go on tour, who will come to New York with you when you have to do a play in New York, or to California if you have to do a film, and who isn't a very strong or scintillating personality, or you have a man who is interesting and demands a lot for himself and for his life—and either you're living completely apart or you're together getting ready to part, and it takes its toll. Stage actresses who marry and have children are often done for as actresses. It takes a lot of strength to come back after you've lost years and lost roles and lost your place, if you had the beginning of one. I know some who never bothered, young actresses who just called it quits. I knew that if the actress died in me, most of what was interesting about me, for myself and for other people—including my husband—

would die with her. On the other hand, I didn't want to destroy the marriage or my child. That's why when I was married to my daughter's father, I mostly did films. Even if I worked for two or three months, I would then have three to six months when I didn't work at all, and I was able to give her a mother. My second marriage was to a producer: he was interested mainly in my bringing home money. I didn't see much of my daughter then, and they were hard years for her. Those years did a lot of damage to us as mother and daughter, and yet they were the years when I played the roles I had so wanted.

The difference between a woman who is an actress and her relationship to her family, and a man who is an actor and his relationship to his family, is, very simply, the difference between a woman and a man. The man is expected to go off to work or to go travelling to earn his living and to provide for everybody, and is not expected to stay at home and take care of the family. But the woman was, when I got married in 1959. Still is, as far as I can see. The child doesn't resent the father going off like that, but deeply resents the mother going off. Never forgives the mother for going off. I don't see that anything has changed between the mother and the child at all. It's going to take more than a constitutional amendment to straighten out small children about equal rights. They may have to be changed from little human beings into little cats and dogs.

Of course my own daughter's father, Rod Steiger, is an actor as well, and until he and I were divorced when Anna was nine, she was really the child of strolling players who lived all over the world. In that way hers is like my own childhood, where we never seemed to be in any one place for more than a year. From the time Anna was three months old until she was thirteen she had a Swiss nurse, Hélène, who looked after her when I was working, and there was always my mother to help us out. Anna was separated a good deal from her father because of his extensive film commitments, but Hélène and my mother and I formed a strong female triumvirate that she could rely on. I enrolled her in a Montessori school as a small child, so that she could transfer within the Montessori system from one country to another; she went to Montessori schools in London, in California, in Paris, in Dublin, and in Rome. When she was old enough I enrolled her in the Lycée, which was formed originally for the children of French diplomats so that they could continue their education wherever their families were posted. Wherever we went there was a Lycée, and she went to it. Consequently this child of strolling players speaks perfect French and fairly good Italian in addition to her English, and in almost any country within a month seems able to pick up enough of the language to speak it. She has interesting friends all over Europe and America, though on the other hand, I believe there is some feeling of rootlessness in her. She's like me in that wherever she is, she thinks the next place is going to be better. Maybe it's my restlessness that made Anna restless, or maybe it was the moving around that she endured when she was so young. Certainly life has always had a bit of excitement for her, because of my career. It's been different from just having Mother at home.

She's never wanted to be an actress, but she does want to be a singer, and that's what she studies at music school. She would like to sing opera, which is performing of a very different order, but still performing. She applies herself to music with enormous strength and to the virtual exclusion of everything else—as I did at her age to the theatre. She seems to have the same driving ambition. I happen to think that the life of an opera singer is more hectic and even less fixed than the life of an actress, and, in that way, worse. You move, you move all the time, and the strain must tell. Still, I would never have reservations about anyone else's doing what they passionately want to do, and I can't think of anything I would rather have for her than a life in music.

I'm sure that the example of an older sister in the theatre—in it, if only vicariously, from about the age of six—has also had its effect upon my brother John. As a boy, it just bored him to death. Those family trips to the Old Vic on Saturdays were often made against his will. But then at school, he briefly wanted at one time to be an actor, and he wasn't bad at it. I remember him in one school play where he wore a grey wig: he was supposed to be an old man and he looked exactly like our grandfather. Following school, he went into the Royal Air Force, and when he got out at twenty he took a job as a script reader at Pinewood Studios. From there he advanced to assistant editor, and soon to editor, and today he's an outstanding film editor. His most recent film is Karel Reisz's *The French Lieutenant's Woman*.

I think that, in part, he advanced as quickly as he did because as a young boy on those Saturday outings he had seen so much fine acting, and knew so much about drama and dramatic performance. He has a good literary mind, he likes music, and above all, he has excellent artistic taste—and I think that much of this came out of the environment that we shared and that was largely created for us by our mother. He has also acquired great technical knowledge of film. How anyone in my family ever got technical knowledge of anything, I don't know. There he was on his own.

Fortunately he wasn't swamped by my sudden fame. He was clever enough to get out by going to boarding school and removing himself from all the clamour. Then he got away from us—my mother and me—by going into the R.A.F. for his national service; he became an officer and emerged, just as the enlistment brochure promises, very much a man. Perhaps all my self-dramatising as a young girl contributed something to his choosing, as his wife, Sheila, a supremely capable woman whose enormous common sense is coupled with great warmth and sensitivity. He may early on have developed a high regard for prudence. He is himself an admirably prudent man.

As for my mother, once the burden of being the keeper of my emotional stability and guardian over my apprenticeship lifted from her, she permitted herself to enjoy her own independence. She bought a houseboat on the Thames, at Chelsea Reach, where she lived for several years until moving into a small house in Chelsea and opening an antique shop there. Our relationship, though still intense and affectionate, has naturally changed with time, and by now I've come to fill for her the roles she once filled for me: protector, adviser, comforter.

⚔ Screen Romance

I for one have had better directors in films than I've had in plays: George Cukor, Tony Richardson, Olivier, Chaplin. Marty Ritt, whom I knew little about before I worked with him, was a big help to me. He directed *The Spy Who Came in from the Cold,* with Burton and me, and *The Outrage,* where I played with Paul Newman. I've enjoyed doing films. I've enjoyed doing them more than I've ever *enjoyed* doing a play. But that doesn't mean they meant as much to me (which may explain why I enjoyed them so). In *The Outrage,* who wouldn't have had a good time? There was Paul Newman being a Mexican and me being a Southern lady, and James Wong Howe making us look terrific charging through the forest on horses—but it had nothing to do with acting. Paul Newman is, in fact, a very fine actor, but that was mostly running around outside having your picture taken. It was simply fun, like going on location. I went all over the place—to New Mexico and Arizona and Spain and Italy and France and Germany and Norway, and that part of it was as exciting as travelling can be, and a great relief from the theatre, which is like a convent or a prison, where the life is narrow and small and generally lonely. Working in the films I got to know all sorts of people and to see all sorts of places and to play all sorts of parts, some of them quite comical for me. The whole thing was rather like "let's pretend," like the kind of playlets children do in the basement on a rainy day. I was a pirate in *The Buccaneer,* an aristocrat in *The Brothers Karamazov,* a Southern beauty in *The Outrage,* a lesbian in *The Haunting,* a nymphomaniac in *The Chapman Report.* But apart from *Limelight, Richard III, Look Back in Anger,* and *The Spy Who Came in from the Cold,* my films haven't added up to anything. I didn't have whatever it takes to be a movie star, and what I had wasn't enough. Then the whole thing didn't have the importance for me, wasn't what I wanted most. And whether I'd wanted it or not, I didn't get it.

It's possible, needless to say, to work well in both films and the theatre. The better the actor, the better the actor. It's possible for Vanessa Redgrave. It's possible for Glenda Jackson. Ralph Richardson is wonderful in both. But as for being a success in films and having films built around you, and building a career in films—for that you must be a movie star. You have to have some ingredient beyond sheer talent, and it isn't only beauty. It's a strong kind of sexual attraction, combined with something that's *recognisable,* something that can't be mistaken, that's you. This may sound vague and simplistic, but what I'm talking about has also to be, necessarily, ineffable. I'm talking about the difference between someone like Joanne Woodward, an excellent actress who has never become a true star, and someone like Audrey Hepburn. Audrey Hepburn was obviously the elfin princess, and Joanne Woodward was nothing *obviously.* And you have to be *something.* An elfin princess. A sad princess. A whore. A taxi driver. A brute. A peasant. Everybody's Cousin Rose. I believe I was supposed to be a lady. On the stage I was an elfin princess—I'm practically still an elfin princess. But in films I fear I was a lady, and that is just fatal to anybody.

The film actor with whom I've had the greatest rapport was Chaplin. Strange, because I was not asked by him to be inventive. I was asked in that film to do what I was told. But I knew I was in the hands of someone who knew what he wanted, and who also had a rather good record. He was the teacher and I was the pupil and he taught me and I did it. It was no more complicated than that. A certain amount of hero worship goes a long way to creating rapport. With Olivier, in *Richard III*, I felt I was working with the greatest actor in the world. I was twenty-two and I had seen his *Richard III* thirteen times at the Old Vic, and there I was playing Lady Anne. I was so enthralled with the idea of working with him and playing this part that it all had tremendous magic before I even started. I don't remember his telling me anything— he didn't have to. I had that rapport with Burton in *Look Back in Anger. We* had it. Your partner just does something that you pick up, and you throw it back to him, and so on. It's the unexpected coming at you while all the time you know that you're *safe*—safe within the other actor's belief in what he's doing and safe within his taste. I once worked with a gentleman who shall be nameless who was always throwing the unexpected at you and it was always wrong. Everything perfectly misjudged. You couldn't react. You stood there in absolute horror. The other actor has to be secure in himself, so secure that he can be interested in *you*. Then the two of you will just start throwing these things back and forth. That is true excitement, a partner who lifts you, who supports you, whom you give to, who gives to you.

As for Hollywood life, it didn't suit me as a person,

so I never got to know if it might have suited me as an actress. When I went there in 1951 to do *Limelight*, I didn't really go to Hollywood, I went to the Chaplin studio. I'd read *Screen Romances* when I was ten years old in Forest Hills, and of course I'd been to the movies. But the idea of Hollywood was vague to me. The place had no reality for me before I got there, and it still had no reality when I left. I'd seen Chaplin's studio and I'd seen Chaplin's world, but that wasn't Hollywood. I met Rita Hayworth once. That was my whole Hollywood. I didn't go back there until six years later to do *The Brothers Karamazov.* I was scared stiff going, mainly because I knew it wasn't going to be Chaplin's studio anymore, with people like James Agee and Clifford Odets and Lion Feuchtwanger, who were the Chaplins' friends and guests. And I was pretty sure it wasn't going to be Dostoyevsky. I got my own apartment just off Beverly Boulevard in Beverly Hills and decided to steel myself and make a go of it. I thought I ought to be in a movie magazine, and so did the producer, and they came and took photographs of me all over this big apartment. I leaned up against things in my sweater, and I opened tin cans in the kitchen, and all I got out of it was an article headlined BRITISH, BUT NOT TEDDIBLY. Spelt with two d's. And with a little crown next to it. I should have got the message then that it just wasn't going to work out for me. But I went on. I thought I ought to go out with everyone who asked me and become a part of the Hollywood night life. I was stunned by it. After about two weeks of going out with the men there, I said I'd never go out with anybody again. I went to nightclubs and I went to the parties and I hated it all. It was very unpleasant. I now had this apartment that I was lonely as hell in. I wanted to be sexy so as to get all these wonderful roles, but I didn't seem able to fool anyone. The wonderful roles just didn't come my way. They went to Jean Simmons, they went to Audrey Hepburn, they went to Natalie Wood. I had an agent who was very nice to me and he had two protégés, me and Shirley MacLaine. It wasn't obvious to me which of us was going to make it—because when I first met Shirley MacLaine I thought, "What a poor plain girl"—but it was obviously apparent to *him*. And Shirley gradually moved in and I gradually moved out. Then I made a new friend, an English actress named Patricia Cutts, and went down to live in Topanga Beach with her. We lived in a kind of two-storey shack. It was an English enclave, really, with Pat and me upstairs, and Patrick Macnee, who's now famous because of television's *The Avengers*, living downstairs. I enjoyed that and so I stayed on to do *The Buccaneer*. But when that was over I left to play in *Duel of Angels* on the London stage and I swore I'd never go back.

I didn't until I was married to Rod Steiger. I went back to live with him there in 1960 and I couldn't get a job. Nobody was interested in me. When I was asked to play a mother in *The Brothers Grimm*, I thought that was the end. I wanted to be a mother but I certainly didn't want to play mothers. That, however, led Marty Ritt to ask me to be in *The Outrage*. Still, I never became a part of the place and the jobs I got came to me through the side door, through personal friendships with Paul Newman and Gore Vidal and Vivien Leigh, and not through anybody calling up and saying, "It's Bloom or nobody." It was stop and start and stop and start. I wanted it to be otherwise because I was stuck living there and I couldn't conceive of living there without working. I wanted it because other people had it and I thought, "Why shouldn't I?" But I never wanted it as an actress. I still don't. It doesn't *mean* anything, I don't know why. It's funny, because it's the only thing that will be left of one. Of course a film dates and in twenty years you look ridiculous. So I don't even know how much of what is left amounts to anything. But it is the only record. And people want it like hell. But I wanted something else.

✕ The Worst of It

The worst of it is being out of work. When you aren't in demand or haven't any job in sight, you suffer a severe loss of self-confidence. This happens to all of the unemployed, but the problem in this profession is that unemployment recurs on a regular basis. It happens to the best of actors as well as to the mediocre. You can be a triumph and win all the prizes, and then you can be out of work for a year. You may be offered parts, but none of them seems right for you, and so you turn them down and wait. This waiting goes on all your life, and it becomes harder as you get older. You feel you should be out there earning your living—I invariably start to think what job I could have, nine to five, on a regular, dependable basis, so that I could bring in a salary and feel necessary to the world. I don't really believe that actors, as a group, need to feel admired and wanted much more than other people; their problem is that the particular uncertainties of the profession put one's character to the test over and over and over. You work like a dog for three months on a television play and the next day you're out on the street with nothing to do. I think that for women it may be less difficult than for men. Most women have a home to run, children and husbands, food and entertaining; it's a job full of day-to-day responsibilities, and in a slack time it takes some of the pain away. But if it goes on too long, then somehow it becomes even worse, because you feel you are disappearing into the house and all your qualities are going down the kitchen drain. It's amazing how self-confidence returns with the offer of a job. You don't even have to be offered King Lear, just something decent that makes you feel necessary, and generally that will restore your faith in yourself until the next time you're out of work.

However, despite the worst of it, I can't imagine myself as something other than an actress, simply because I don't think I have any other capability on a first-class level. I can imagine having been much happier if I had been able to do something else. I can imagine having been better educated than my narrow pursuit of a career allowed for. I can imagine having become more tolerant and worldly, having become more generally inquisitive sooner rather than later, had I not been idealistic about my "art" to a degree that was idiotic. If I had the same outlook now that I did when I was twenty, I'd have to be put away in a lunatic asylum. I can imagine having had a better life with men had I not been a young girl who'd grown up like a novitiate in the theatre, as cloistered a world for me as any convent school. And I can imagine being much happier now in some profession that offers increasingly greater satisfactions as you get older, rather than the reverse. In acting, as you get older the parts get fewer—films die out for nearly every actress after forty, and you can count on your fingers the number of important stage roles there are for mature women. I would have liked to be in a profession where, when you reach your full maturity and are at the height of your powers, *everything* is there for you to do, rather than it all going away.

In part I started to write this book because I wondered if I did regret having been cast in the role of an actress so very early in life as never to have had the opportunity to find out if I could do or be anything else. I wanted to find out what had made me do it, and really, I'm no nearer an answer now than when I started. I don't see how it could have turned out otherwise. I was just this peculiar little girl who couldn't think of anything else. Nobody had to push me into it and nobody did. I didn't need boyfriends and school friends and the social life and all the other things that ordinarily go with being young and English and middle class. All I needed was what I got. And understanding that does away with every regret.

DIANA COOPER

Philip Ziegler

Philip Ziegler's bestselling biography tells the story of Lady Diana Cooper – beautiful, witty, outrageous, generous ... the idol of a golden generation.

'Combines total honesty with total affection ... a portrait which you can laugh over, cry over and think over as well' – *Punch*

'No wonder Evelyn Waugh loved her' – *Scotsman*

'For nine decades a symbol of all that is dashing and daring, a synonym for courage and wit and inspired friendship' – *Sunday Telegraph*

CLINGING TO THE WRECKAGE

John Mortimer

'The sunniest and funniest memoir since Clive James' – Claire Tomalin in the *Sunday Times*

'Enchantingly witty ... should be held as the model for all autobiographies of our times. England would be a poor place without Mr Mortimer' – Auberon Waugh

The creator of Rumpole, the best playwright to ever appear for a murderer at the Central Criminal Court, the son who immortalized a parent in *A Voyage Round My Father*, John Mortimer now gives us his funny, stringent and tender autobiography.

'Exhilarating ... hilarious ... repays reading for its wisdom and depth ... His evocation of his parents is one of the most remarkable things in modern writing' – *Sunday Times*

AN ACTOR AND HIS TIME

John Gielgud

In *An Actor and His Time* John Gielgud tells the story of his life in the theatre – a story already enjoyed by millions of radio listeners and which tells of the plays he starred in and directed, and of the actors and actresses he knew. And, as the curtain rises on Ellen Terry, on Sarah Bernhardt, on Mrs Patrick Campbell, Sir Ralph Richardson, Richard Burton and many others, sixty glorious years of British theatre unfold before our eyes.

'Much more than a recital of a great actor's career, it is a lively history of our theatre from Edwardian times to the present, told with wit, wisdom and humour' – *The Times Educational Supplement*

UP IN THE CLOUDS, GENTLEMEN PLEASE

John Mills

'It is a rare pleasure to read such a happy book by one who is so justifiably happy in all respects' – Laurence Olivier

From the early beginnings hard at music hall song-and-dance-routines to the days of *Cavalcade* and *Jill, Darling*, to the film epics – *In Which We Serve, Ice Cold in Alex, Scott of the Antarctic*, to the prized Oscar for *Ryan's Daughter*, this is a heartwarming story of fame and fortune, of true love, lasting friendships and of a happy and united acting family.

Drama, farce and tragedy – not to mention some spectacular falls – have all had their part in a life that is as varied as it is successful. Marvellously honest, affectionate, funny and wise, *Up in the Clouds, Gentlemen Please* is a stupendous read.

WAYS OF ESCAPE

Graham Greene

The second part of his acclaimed autobiography, which began in *A Sort of Life*.

From Haiti under Papa Doc, Vietnam in the last days of the French, Kenya during the Mau Mau, and Hollywood, to the making of *The Third Man* in Vienna and his time in the British Secret Service, Graham Greene writes exquisitely of people and places, of faith, doubt, fear and of the craft of writing, as he found himself repeatedly at 'the dangerous edge of things'.

'Marvellously rich' – William Trevor

A BETTER CLASS OF PERSON

John Osborne

'This passionate and aggressive self-portrait of the artist as dandy, guerrilla, malingerer, society fox and family cad ... triumphs, in the belief that life is more extravagant and extra-ordinary than art' – Michael Ratcliffe in *The Times*

'Splendidly enjoyable ... an honest, beautifully written account of a stultifying childhood and early adventures in the provincial theatre' – John Mortimer in the *Sunday Times* Books of the Year

'Wonderfully funny about the horrors of digs, backstage skimble-skamble and awful Home Counties comedies or farces about maids compromised in their cami-knickers ... by far the best thing he has written' – John Barber in the *Daily Telegraph*

'Written with great gusto ... a lovely book. It has jokes. It is not mellow. And it constantly brings alive that remotest of periods, the recent past' – Alan Bennett in the *London Review of Books*

NANCY CUNARD

Anne Chisholm

The only child of an American society hostess and an English baronet, Nancy Cunard became the darling of high-café society in the twenties and thirties. She knew T. S. Eliot, James Joyce and Louis Aragon; she sat for Cecil Beaton and Max Beerbohm sketched her; she was an Aldous Huxley heroine in *Antic Hay*. She was also a poet and a publisher, a passionate advocate of racial equality and a journalist in the Spanish Civil War. By the time of her tragic death in 1965, Nancy Cunard had become the dazzling symbol of her age.

'Excellently written and compulsively readable' – Auberon Waugh in *The New York Times Book Review*

MOKSHA

Aldous Huxley

In these collected writings the creator of *Brave New World* explores the brave new dawn of the psychedelic mind-changing drugs, mescalin and LSD. With the lucid appraisal of the philosopher, the reverent curiosity of the mystic and the clinical detachment of the scientist, he discusses their political, medical and ethical implications; and, with the eloquence of the poet and the power of the visionary, he describes his own experience of them, in the fullness of life and at the hour of his death.

CHARMED LIVES

Michael Korda

The story of Alexander Korda and the fabulous Korda film dynasty starring Garbo, Dietrich, Churchill and a cast of thousands.

'Charmed lives, doubly charmed book ... Comments, jokes, experiences; and at the heart of it all there is Alexander Korda, powerful, brilliant, extravagant, witty, charming. And fortunate: fortunate in his biographer. Few men have the luck to be written about with so personal an appreciation, so amused, yet so deep an affection' – Dilys Powell in *The Times*

THE LIFE OF NOËL COWARD

Cole Lesley

'*The Life of Noël Coward* is – to borrow Coward's own description of his life – "fabulously enjoyable": a graceful and glistening piece of biography, reading which is like a holiday in a rented Rolls' – Kenneth Tynan in the *Observer*

'Funny, sad, witty, bawdy and totally unputdownable, it sheds new light on its many splendoured subject and enshrines for all time several decades of social history. I loved it!' – Peta Fordham in *The Times*

EDWARD VII

Christopher Hibbert

'His biography of the King has been worth waiting for ... Among the most versatile of living historians, he combines impeccable scholarship with a liveliness of style that lures the reader from page to page' – Kenneth Rose in the *Sunday Telegraph*

'Wholly admirable ... wonderfully well illustrated, highly readable and in places extremely funny ... His character is vividly portrayed – the charm, the courtesy, the sudden outbursts of rage, the endless fuss about clothes, medals and uniforms, the perpetual fear of *ennui*, the heavy banter, the practical jokes ... the ceaseless amours ... I can imagine no better a present for someone who, unlike its subject, reads books' – Robert Blake in the *Spectator*

CLEMENTINE CHURCHILL

Mary Soames

Lady Soames describes her book as 'a labour of love – but I trust not of blind love'; others have acclaimed it as one of the outstanding biographies of the decade:

'Perceptive and affectionate, shrewd and tender ... a joy to read' – Elizabeth Longford

'Lady Soames has carried out the extremely delicate and difficult task of writing the real story of her mother. I found it particularly moving because I had a very deep affection for her father and mother' – Harold Macmillan

'A triumph ... her subject, unknown yet well-known, is enthralling' – Eric James in *The Times*

ABOUT TIME

Penelope Mortimer

Winner of the Whitbread Award

Her ironic and delightful autobiography of girlhood between the wars. After leaving her fifth school, Penelope Mortimer was sent to train as a secretary, but soon moved on, via London University and Bloomsbury, to marriage and the birth of her first daughter in Hitler's Vienna. On the outbreak of war, she celebrated her twenty-first birthday in the Café de Paris – 'we drank champagne to the present and future, but not to the past, that I have tried to celebrate here'.

'It goes down not so much like a madeleine as like a lemon water-ice on a hot day, sharp and gritty as well as smooth and sweet . . . leaving a taste for more' – *Listener*

MEMORIES OF A CATHOLIC GIRLHOOD

Mary McCarthy

'There is an element of *tour de force* in this brilliant book' – *Observer*

Blending memories and family myths, Mary McCarthy takes us back to the twenties, when she was orphaned into a world of relations as colourful, potent and mysterious as the Catholic religion. From her black-veiled Jewish grandmother to her wicked Uncle Myers who beat her for the good of her soul, here are the people who inspired her devastating sense of the sublime and ridiculous, and her witty, novelist's imagination.

GEORGE ORWELL: A LIFE

Bernard Crick

'A triumph of the first order' – Michael Foot in the *New Standard*

'It is hardly worth using up space to declare just how good it is. Different readers will come away from its seventeen pungent and packed chapters with diverse memories of its excellence' – Peter Sedgwick in the *Guardian*

'Crick has a remarkable independent mind and a large, irascible way of seeing things' – Noël Annan in the *New York Review of Books*

'Crick's analytical mind, combined with his mastery of the historical background and context, make him the ideal guide' – Arthur Koestler in the *Observer*

'Assured and eloquent . . . In its own uncompromised integrity it is both monumental and appealing' – *Los Angeles Times*

Winner of the 1980 Yorkshire Post Book of the Year Award

MY LIFE WITH NYE

Jennie Lee

His wife for over twenty years, Jennie Lee narrates the story of Aneurin Bevan's stormy career, revealing a man who was not only a national figure but also a philosopher and poet.

'Intelligent, often penetrating, gossipy, tough, lively and warm . . . I couldn't put it down' – *Guardian*

'Her writing has much of the verve of her conversation, fresh, natural, brightened with sudden sparkles of wit, and abounding in wicked perceptions of human frailties . . . essential reading' – Jill Craigie in *The Times*